Is This Bottle Corked?

Also by Kathleen Burk

Old World, New World: The Story of Britain and America
Troublemaker: The Life and History of A. J. P. Taylor
Morgan Grenfell 1838–1988: The Biography of a Merchant Bank

Also by Michael Bywater

The Chronicles of Bargepole
Lost Worlds: What Have We Lost, and Where Did It Go?
Big Babies: Or: Why Don't We Just Grow Up?

Is This Bottle Corked?

HARMONY BOOKS
New York

kathleen burk AND
michael bywater

THE SECRET LIFE OF WINE

Published in the United States by Harmony Books, an imprint of the Crown
Publishing Group, a division of Random House, Inc., New York.
www.crownpublishing.com

Harmony Books is a registered trademark and the Harmony Books colophon
is a trademark of Random House, Inc.
Originally published in Great Britain by Faber and Faber Limited,
London, in 2008.

Grateful acknowledgment is made to the Estates of Michael Flanders
and Donald Swann for permission to reprint an excerpt from
"M'Deira M'Dear" by Michael Flanders and Donald Swann.
Reprinted by permission of the Estates of Michael Flanders
and Donald Swann, leonberger@donaldswann.co.uk.

Library of Congress Cataloging-in-Publication Data is available upon request.

ISBN 978-0-307-46291-6

Printed in the United States of America

DESIGN BY ELINA D. NUDELMAN
PHOTO BY CHRISTINA B. CASTRO

10 9 8 7 6 5 4 3 2 1

First U.S. Edition

For Howard Hyman, expander of the palate:
may his cellar flourish
and
for Michael Jewess, provider of some of the words, many
of the numbers, and most of the science

CONTENTS

INTRODUCTION

Where do we begin?

If this were a book about what wine to drink with what food, it would be easy. If this were a book about what wine to buy to impress your friends and/or business associates, it would still be easy. If this were a learned volume on the effect of the phylloxera aphid on the French wine industry, it would probably be easier still.

But this is none of those books. It is, rather, to wine writing what the cabinet of bibelots was to Edwardian interior decorating: a collection of, one hopes, charming diversions to catch the eye, divert the mind, and perhaps provoke conversation. When you read the tale of the weeping sommelier, or consider "comet wines," or spend a moment considering potlatch, wine diamonds, Hippocrene, *terroir*, or gout, there is nothing that we want you to *do*. All we would like is for that part of your mind that is occupied with good living in general, and wine in particular (which may be a large or a small proportion of your mind, according to personal disposition), to be diverted, entertained, and primed with the sort of curiosities that make human society so much fun.

Yet again, where do we begin? Wine is perhaps more profoundly dug into—or poured out upon—human history than any other artifact, natural or man-made. Its history stretches back perhaps eight thousand years; certainly, it makes its appearance in the first written story we now possess, the four-thousand-year-old Sumerian *Epic of Gilgamesh*, which comes from what is now Iraq and was then the Kingdom Between the Rivers, Mesopotamia, the cradle of civilization. There the king's friend is told by a temple slave to drink seven goblets of wine; there King Gilgamesh himself encounters

> *the woman of the vines*
> *Siduri the maker of wine.*
> *She lives beside the sea;*
> *She sits in her gardens by the sea's edge*
> *Her golden bowl and golden vats given by the gods,*
> *Veiled . . .*

Where there are grapes, there is wine; where there is wine, almost without exception, it is not only a source of good fellowship but a crucial symbol of ritual. At Jewish weddings, the bride and  groom drink the *kiddushin* wine from two goblets and the *nisuin* wine from one, symbolizing the union of the couple. Timothy is encouraged to "drink no longer water, but use a little wine for thy stomach's sake and thine often infirmities." Jesus of Nazareth transformed water into wine at Cana, and blessed it at the Last Supper (the *kiddush*, or dedication of the wine to Elohim, begins each Sabbath meal); and in almost every Christian community the action is repeated and remembered to this day in the communion prayers or the Canon of the Roman Catholic Mass. Wine was consecrated in sacramental banquets of the Roman temples of Mithras; it is found in Hindu ceremonials; it is one of the great subjects of the *Rubá'iyát of Omar Khayyám* who, in Edward FitzGerald's ecstatic translation, sings of

> *divine*
> *High-piping Péhlevi, with "Wine! Wine! Wine!*
> *Red Wine!"—the Nightingale cries to the Rose*

Hard to imagine such paeans to beer, or liturgies celebrated in gin and tonic, however fine. Not that we would go so far as the medieval Germans, who regarded beer as the drink of pagans and barbarians, while wine represented civilization and Christianity; nor would we join forces with Hilaire Belloc, who claimed that beer was the drink of the dull Protestant north, wine the libation of the exuberant Catholic south. He has been often misquoted as declaring:

> *Wherever the Catholic sun doth shine,*
> *There's always laughter and good red wine.*
> *At least I've always found it so.*
> *Benedicamus Domino!*

though what he actually wrote was:

> *But Catholic men that live upon wine*
> *Are deep in the water, and frank, and fine;*
> *Wherever I travel I find it so,*
> *Benedicamus Domino.*

Whatever he wrote, though (and he wrote, too, of "The fleas that tease in the High Pyrenees / And the wine that tasted of tar"), the truth remains that wine has bathed humankind in its benevolent light (scarlet or golden, according to your choice) throughout history. The Rotarians or Freemasons indulging in their ceremonial "taking of wine" join hands across the centuries with the guests at the Greek symposia, gathered round the krater with its formalized wine-and-water admixture; the breaking of a wine bottle on the prow of a new ship echoes the pagan libations poured out to the gods. Wherever we turn, there is wine. There it is, in the flasks of Roman soldiers, far from home, to flavor and sterilize the alien waters (and they grew vines, too, in the north of England and—you can still see the vineyard terraces—in the Cotswolds). Here it is in Shakespeare: Falstaff calling for more sack, the Duke of Clarence drowned in a malmsey butt. Here is Cleopatra, famed (but *did* she? *Could* she have?) for dissolving a pearl in her wine to impress her wealth and power upon Mark Antony. Here are at least three notable wine connoisseurs among the Founding Fathers of the United States of America, while over there sits great Dionysos, the god of wine, of fertility and collective joy, in whose name the classical Athenians held their festival of tragedy, the *tragoedia,* or "goat-songs" of the City Dionysia, attended by all citizens.

However, the discoveries of Louis Pasteur—that wine was a living thing, made *by* living things, those benevolent yeasts— may have affected winemaking; however it may have become more predictable, perhaps in some cases more industrialized, wine itself will never be a truly industrial product like vodka or mass-produced beers. Nobody will ever wonder about the story locked in a glass of Bud Lite or the hidden narrative of a rum and Coke, but there are few wines that do not (if one is in a fanciful mood) murmur up from the glass, speaking to the attentive drinker of land and fruit and hope and human labor. Wine, more than any other food or drink, is a storyteller, and it is some of its more off-beat stories that we hope to tell in this book: stories of emperors and gods, of bugs and rituals, of organ pipes and astronomy and raisins and forgetfulness.

The habit of looking for the story in a glass of wine is one easily acquired and never forgotten. It pleases the mind and amuses one's friends. It changes, for the beginner, the nature of wine from a thorny path, a nest of vipers, a sort of obstacle course of snobberies and faux pas, into an affable and sympathetic narrative for every taste and disposition. We smell our wine; we taste it, and examine its color and clarity. We should also, perhaps, listen to what it has to say about itself.

And, of course, drink it. There was a Greek restaurant in London's Camden Town, now long gone, that served ordinary Greek wines in ordinary drinking tumblers, without ceremony. It stood in contrast to its more chic counterparts in the posher parts of town, where sommeliers, dignified as bishops, hovered over the nervous diner performing arcane rituals with corkscrew and tastevin, cork and napkin. On its menus was printed a motto: *A meal without wine is like a day without sunshine.* Alas, in London then, both were the rule rather than the exception. But we learned. Since then, country after country has developed, improved, and exported its wines. Cases, bottles, barrels now crisscross the oceans in a benevolent globalization. We drink more wine than ever before, whether the doctors say that (this week) it will leave us demented or (next week) that it is the secret of spry longevity. The fruit of the vine and the skill of the winemaker have between them the secret of an immemorial magic. But, like magic, it's not enough just to read about it. It is necessary to experience it, in moderation but often.

To accompany this little book, we suggest a *premier cru* Pauillac, or possibly a crisp young *vinho verde*. Or maybe a flinty Greco di Tufo or a vintage champagne, or a South American Tannat or a Klein Constantia or something from a Provençal co-op, dispensed from a petrol-pump nozzle into your waiting jerry can, or . . . or . . . or whatever you like. Draw the cork, open the book, and *bon appetit*.

We will leave the last word to the poet Peter Meinke's "Advice to My Son":

> *Therefore, marry a pretty girl*
> *after seeing her mother;*
> *show your soul to one man,*
> *work with another,*
> *and always serve bread with your wine.*

> *But, son,*
> *always serve wine.*

NOTE: A collaborative book like this will often refer to something one of its authors did, or saw, or drank. It would be tiresome to say "I [Kathleen]" or "I [Michael]" every time. And so we have used "we" in every case. It's easier on the eye. But it doesn't mean we were both there. And it's certainly not the royal "we."

Metonymy, morphic resonance, and sommeliers, or, is this wine corked?

WE, THE AUTHORS, would not so much as *contemplate* physical violence toward wine waiters. We do, however, send wine back, sometimes because it is corked. At this point, we note that corking or cork taint is a fault of the *wine*, not of the bottle. Our title, therefore, relies on the figure of speech (subclass trope) metonymy, in which, according to our dictionary, "the name of one thing is put for that of another related to it . . . as 'the bottle' for 'drink.'" Our title came before our dictionary research, and we are now convinced that our choice of words is an example of morphic resonance as proposed by Rupert Sheldrake, whereby existing patterns influence future ones merely by existing.

There are, of course, ways of arresting the attention of sommeliers other than by throwing a bottle at them. To ensure their respect, we suggest the following dos and don'ts:

Do send a wine back, saying that it is corked, if it has the characteristic musty smell that resembles mushrooms or the result of striding through the dead leaves of woodlands in the autumn. If the sommelier has sniffed the cork after pulling it, he ought to have already spotted it for you; you might then look him straight in the eye in an inquiring manner as you suggest that it is corked.

Don't use the term *corked* to refer to any other fault in wine.

Do send back white wine if it is oxidized or maderized (see p. 46), in which oxygen has managed to slip into the wine through the cork, turned it a dark yellow, and given it an aroma resembling madeira.

Don't say that a wine is faulty because it has left a deposit in the glass; it may indicate that the winemaker expects his customers to know that the deposit is harmless and to appreciate his reluctance to risk wine quality with the rather drastic processes of tartrate stabilization.

What *is* corking? The chemical compound 2,4,6-trichloroanisole (TCA for short) is blamed for the corking of wine and is produced by the action of fungi on cork in the presence of chlorine. The fight between the proponents of screw caps and of corks is bitter (see p. 86), and cork taint is the main battleground. A screw cap eliminates the main source of TCA contamination in wine, but also that frisson of excitement when the cork is pulled and you sniff for mushrooms and autumnal woodlands, wondering whether the wine will be drinkable.

Yes, but what exactly *is* wine?

THE FIRST THING any European should do, when trying to find out what anything is, is to ask Brussels: the European Union will have a definition of and a regulation for it. For example, Council Regulation (EC) No. 1493/1999 of May 17, 1999, on the common regulation of the market in wine, says:

> WINE: the product obtained exclusively from the total or partial alcoholic fermentation of fresh grapes, whether or not crushed, or of grape must. (Annex I, paragraph 10)

Two more definitions are needed in order to understand this one:

> FRESH GRAPES: the fruit of the vine used in making wine, ripe or even slightly raisined, which may be crushed or

pressed by normal wine-cellar means and which may spontaneously produce alcoholic fermentation. (Annex I, paragraph 1)

This has a certain circularity.

GRAPE MUST: the liquid product obtained naturally or by physical processes from fresh grapes. (Annex I, paragraph 2)

Does *obtained naturally* mean crushing the grapes with naked feet?

Vine in the definition of fresh grapes refers to Article 19, which says that only varieties of *Vitis vinifera* and crosses thereof with other species of *Vitis* may be entered into the classification, and that "areas planted with vine varieties for the purpose of wine production not entered into the classification shall be grubbed up." This is seen as ensuring both the quality and the "typicity" of grapes that will be made into wine in any locality. But it also sets out clearly who would be allowed to receive any of the subsidies Brussels may be proffering: only those who restrict themselves to the permitted varieties. This also forbids the use of any native American varieties of grapes—and, given their quality (see p. 137), this is just as well. Also rejected is wine made from any other fruits. So elderberry wine (alas for the English) and dandelion wine (alas for fans of Ray Bradbury) are merely "alcoholic beverages."

So: applause for the European regulator in trying to maintain the quality of European wine, but no gold star to Brussels for the drafting of legal documents.

So who first invented wine?

AS WITH ALL successful products, there is a clamor of voices claiming its invention. Yet it is probably more to the point to ask, who first discovered wine? It is not difficult to make it. On the outside skin of the grape is the yeast and on the inside is the juice: mix them together, leave it to ferment for a few days, and the result is wine. All you really need are grapes.

One claimant is Noah. After he and his family had descended from the ark onto dry land, the Lord told them to replenish the earth. According to Genesis chapter 9, verses 20–21:

And Noah began *to be* an husbandman, and he planted a vineyard: And he drank of the wine, and was drunken; and he was uncovered within his tent.

What is interesting here is the statement that he planted a vineyard, because the earliest wine would have been made from wild grapes; indeed, why plant a vineyard if you do not know what you can do with the produce? Perhaps, instead, he was the first viticulturalist? A subsidiary question is, why did he get drunk? Had he not anticipated the effect of the wine? Or perhaps the effect was just what he wanted after a hard day's work. Medieval glosses on these verses, and particularly on verse 21, reflect a wide range of opinions on the subject.

For the ancient Greeks, the discovery of wine by men was the gift of Dionysos, the god of wine, the avatar who burst out of Thrace—or perhaps Phrygia—and brought the knowledge of wine to Attica. He disclosed the secret to a peasant called Icarios and his daughter Erigone, with whom he had lodged as a guest: the gift was his return for their hospitality. However, he commanded Icarios that, once he had successfully made wine, he was to teach the skill to others; the outcome was disastrous. Icarios shared his wine with a group of shepherds, who drank a very great deal and, unaccustomed to the effect it had on them, feared that Icarios had poisoned them. They grabbed their clubs and beat him to death. When his daughter returned, she looked for him in vain, and it was only when his faithful dog Moera led her to where her father had been buried that she realized what had happened. In despair, she hanged herself. But Dionysos rewarded them: Icarios became the star Boötes, his daughter was transformed into the constellation Virgo, and Moera became Canis or Sirius, the Dog Star. (Boötes has another title, "the grape gatherer," because it rises in the autumn at the time of the vintage.) In truth, the vine was widely cultivated by the early Bronze Age—both Homer and Hesiod make it clear that wine was an essential part of life—and clay tablets dating from the late Bronze Age (about 1200 BC) connect Dionysos with wine, providing early evidence for his cult.

Another candidate for the discoverer of wine is a lady of the harem of the Persian king Jamshíd. The king greatly enjoyed eating grapes and caused them to be stored in jars so that he could enjoy them year round. One day it was discovered that the grapes were no longer sweet—in fact, they had fermented, a process unknown to the king and his household. He feared that the liquid was poisonous, and thus had the jar labeled "poison." The lady in question was bedeviled with migraine headaches that caused her terrible pain and had lost the will to live, so she drank deeply of the "poison." Sinking to the floor, she slept without dreams and without pain, and when she finally awoke, she felt refreshed as she had not felt for weeks without number. She returned to the jar and finished its contents. She was found out, however, and was forced to tell the king what she had done. Curious, he had a quantity of the wine made, and when it was finished, it was drunk with pleasure by the king and all his court. This Persian legend has some plausibility. By the use of microchemical techniques on archaeological residues found at Hajji Firuz Tepe, it has become clear that wine was being produced in the highlands of northeastern Persia in the Neolithic Period (c. 5400 BC).

The primary competitor is the Transcaucasus, particularly in what is now Georgia. Strictly speaking, however, it was ancient

Armenia, which in classical times included much of eastern Turkey, Azerbaijan, and Georgia. The vine was indigenous to the Armenian valleys, having established itself there over a million years ago, and petrified grape pips have been found at several Neolithic sites in the Caucasus on the Black Sea side. Other archaeological evidence from later periods includes irrigation channels, wine chambers with processing equipment, and large clay jugs. In Georgia itself, wine has been a dominant part of the culture for over five thousand years. Certainly there is ample archaeological evidence of this, with special knives for pruning dating back to between 3000 and 2000 BC and vessels from Neolithic sites dating to at least 7000 BC. A conclusion might be that, although the discovery of wine and then the making of wine occurred in a number of different places, at this point Georgia seems to be the winner, in terms of both the longevity and the pervasiveness of its wine culture: when Christianity arrived in Georgia in the fourth century, the first cross was made of vines.

Will you be needing grapes for that?

CONSIDERING Dr. Johnson's definition of wine—the fermented juice of the grape (see p. 93)—and in contrast with the EU diktat, we might pause to ask ourselves what else wine can legitimately, though possibly ill-advisedly, be made of other than grapes. Mead—which will crop up again later (see p. 108)—springs to mind, though it's a bit of a stretch to consider honey a vegetable. But the truth is that it's hard to find anything that grows that *hasn't* at some time or another been made into something that might be described as wine.

We have before us as we write detailed instructions for the making of carrot wine, "corn squeezins," cucumber wine, wine from Jerusalem artichokes, onion wine, pea wine, peapod wine, parsnip wine, wine from pumpkins, wine from zucchini, sweet potato wine, sugarcane wine, and tomato wine. Most alarming of all, here is a recipe that begins:

> Put water on to boil. Shred Brussels sprouts and place in primary. Chop raisins and add to primary. When water boils, pour over cabbage and raisins. Add sugar, stirring to dissolve. Let sit overnight.

Brussels sprout wine. But sprouts are famously among the three things—the others being eggs and asparagus—that *do not go* with wine. All we require now is asparagus wine and wine made from eggs, and we will have the top three self-canceling wines imaginable. Admittedly, the supplier of this recipe, Roxanne's Wine Cellar, begins with a disclaimer:

> I developed this recipe by request. A search of the Internet for a Brussels Sprout Wine recipe only yielded a note on a website that there are no recipes on the Web for Brussels sprout wine!

But who would request such a thing? And surely the exclamation mark at the end, suggesting surprise at the absence of such a recipe on the Internet, is completely inexplicable.

However, *de gustibus non est disputandum*—a Latin phrase meaning "there's no accounting for taste," useful to deploy when someone turns up for dinner bearing a bottle of homemade Brussels sprout wine.

Apple wine, pear wine, bilberry wine, cherry wine, elderflower wine, ginger wine, coriander wine, plum wine: if it grows, if it produces sugar (or if it can have sugar added to it), someone, somewhere, will have produced wine from it, even if only once.

But why the unquestioned supremacy of *real* wine, by which we mean (siding with Dr. Johnson's first definition and that of the EU) wine made from grapes?

It used to be a mystery. Why should grapes be superior to strawberries, peaches, or rhubarb? There seems inherently no reason—or there did not until 1998, when a Cornell scientist, Robert Kime, came up with what appears to be a very good reason.

It's the other thing about wine that's the problem. The alcohol.

Grape-based wines can be allowed to develop an alcohol content of up to 14.5 percent and still be considered excellent by many. But the aromatic compounds in other fruits and vegetables are less robust, and alcohol is, after all, a solvent. Allow the percentage of alcohol to rise to 11 percent, and the aromatics will be dissolved and evaporate literally overnight.

The answer? Halt fermentation at about 10.5 percent alcohol by refrigeration to 28°F.

And now we wish we had never repeated this information, lest it encourage anyone to make a Brussels sprout wine that captures the true, the unspeakable flavors of the things.

How did wine help Marduk become king of the Gods?

THE BABYLONIAN creation epic *Enûma Elish* tells how Marduk, "the bull calf of the sun" and a young but mighty storm god, vanquished and destroyed Tiamat, the great mother goddess of Sumer. Tiamat and her son and consort Kingu, an evil pair, were the sea dragons of Chaos. Marduk was inclined to indulge in pranks, such as putting the winds on a leash, and a number of the lesser gods grew resentful. They decided to ask Tiamat to destroy him. She in turn decided to make war on Marduk and on those gods who were her enemies and who supported him. She created eleven monsters and put Kingu at the head of her forces. Her enemies wanted her destroyed, but who was to lead their forces? She was so powerful that none wished to go into battle against her. In desperation Ea, the god of wisdom and father of Marduk, decided that his son had the best chance of defeating her. Therefore, he asked Marduk to fight her as the champion of her enemies. Marduk

> opened his mouth, saying unto [Ea], "If I indeed, as your
> avenger,
> Am to vanquish Tiamat and save your lives,
> Set up the Assembly, proclaim supreme my destiny!"

In short, the assembly of the gods had to agree that if he won, he would be their chief forever.

This would be difficult: in general the gods would be loath to concede supreme power to any of their number, let alone to a young god. Ea decided that he should invite the gods who were the enemies of Tiamat to a banquet. He had his servants prepare mounds of pancakes, a favorite food of the Mesopotamian gods, and placed beside each of them a huge vessel brimming with a fragrant and delicious wine—or alcoholic beverage—made from dates. To encourage their drinking, he gave each god a tube through which he could drink his wine without needing to move. To encourage their relaxation, he had musicians play soft music on their pipes, and he brought into the hall many sheep, whose bleating further lulled the gods into restfulness. When the time came for the gods to vote on Marduk's proposal, the entire assembly agreed to his terms.

Arming himself with bow and arrows, a bludgeon of thunder, and a flail of lightning, the young storm god marched against the ancient goddess. One by one he defeated her monsters, and after a terrible battle he destroyed her and imprisoned the monsters in the bowels of the earth. He then tore the body of Tiamat into two pieces. He flung one piece up into the air, which formed the firmament; the other piece became the foundation of the earth.

The losing gods were punished by being forced to serve the other gods, digging the earth and sowing the crops. They eventually rebelled, burning their baskets and spades. Marduk killed Kingu and used his blood and bones to create a puppet, man, to do all of the work. In gratitude, the gods built the city of Babylon, the center of worship of Marduk as the leader of the pantheon of the gods of the Babylonian Empire.

What is *terroir*, and should we care?

TERROIR is one of those words that can only be translated by a sentence. For the more mystical among French winemakers and their equivalents in other countries, it is almost the spirit of the place, incorporating any and everything that makes up or influences a vineyard. Let us imagine that you want to buy a good vineyard, and, after due consideration of what is on offer—both in the market and in your bank account—you visit your choice. Stand in the middle of it: what do you see and feel? There's the climate, for one. In fact, it's for three, because grape growers divide it into macroclimate, which covers a region; mesoclimate, which covers a vineyard; and microclimate, which covers a vine. Is it hot, warm, cool, or cold, or a combination? Then there's the soil: what is it made of, and can water drain through it easily—most vines prefer keeping their feet dry—but can it retain just enough water for when the vine needs it? There's the altitude: is it high up or low down? There's the aspect: is it on a hillside—often better—or on flat land? How many hours of sunlight does a season provide, and how much warmth does the vineyard retain at night? Are there small rocks that are heated during the day and then radiate this warmth onto the vines at night? Is it near bodies of water, which moderate the heat or cold? In short, *terroir* refers to all of the natural elements of a place. This means that the place matters. Furthermore, it means that some places are better than others. And most of all, it means that wines made from grapes grown in the best *terroirs* can command much higher prices than those wines made by less fortunate proprietors.

Many growers and winemakers in the New World continue to deny that such a thing exists. Some years ago, a California farmer reputedly insisted that it is all just dirt: give the winemaker the grapes and he or she will make good wine. Certainly, size can make a difference as to whether or not you have a *terroir* to celebrate, in that the owner of a thousand-acre ranch in Australia spread out over a flat terrain is more likely to dismiss the concept than the Burgundian owner of four hectares whose soil differs markedly from that of the vineyard across the road. Nevertheless, it is the case that increasing numbers of New World winemakers are now, rightly, insisting on the quality of their own *terroirs*.

So the real question is not "What is terroir?" but "Does terroir matter?" Except for the wrapped-up and blindfolded, it must be clear to any human being that *terroir* exists. After all, why plant grapes in one field, cotton in another, and wheat in another? It is because the conditions are right for the respective crops. Can the winemaker really overcome obstacles provided by grapes that are not quite ripe, relatively tasteless, or too watery? If he wants to provide a drinkable wine, probably so. If she wants to produce a premium wine, almost certainly not. In other words, is great wine made in the vineyard or in the winery? Will you as an owner pay more for a great vineyard or a great winemaker? If you want to make a great wine, you must first acquire the great vineyard. Without that, even a great winemaker will struggle to make a great wine. To maintain both your vineyard and your winemaker, you need your wine to command a great price. And therefore, across the world, all those who aspire to this position celebrate their unique *terroirs*.

Desire makes believers of us all.

Why did Omar Khayyám write so much about wine?

CONSIDERING that he was one of the greatest mathematicians of the medieval period (he lived from 1042 to 1131) as well as a notable astronomer and philosopher, why did Omar Khayyám write so much about wine? As a mathematician, he has exerted an influence that still exists today. His treatise on the theory of Euclid's *Elements* advanced the theory of numbers, but of even more fundamental importance, in his mid-twenties he wrote a famous treatise on algebra, demonstrating, for the first time, how to solve cubic equations. Remember quadratic equations from school (e.g., $x^2 - 5x + 6 = 0$, which is solved by $x = 2$ or $x = 3$)? Khayyám was the first to show how one would solve cubic equations such as $x^3 + 5x^2 + 3x - 81 = 0$ (of which one solution is $x = 3$). But this was not enough: hidden for years from all but his circle of friends, he was a poet—and not only a poet, but a Persian poet who did not conform to Islam.

Islam had been brought to Persia by the Arabs in 642, barely ten years after the death of the Prophet. In northeast Persia, where Khayyám was born, the orthodox principles of Islamic law were determinedly enforced. Islam forbade its followers from drinking wine, a prohibition strengthened in the eleventh and twelfth centuries by the growth of religious factions, many of which were fanatical in support of their beliefs. Omar ibn Ibrahim al-Khayyám—Omar the son of Ibrahim the tentmaker—was nominally a Muslim, but he was secular in his bones and had little time for turbulent religious controversies. Nevertheless, it was safer to wear an outward conformity, and the *ruba'i* provided a vehicle with which to express his disdain.

The *ruba'i* was a two-line stanza of Persian poetry set out as a quatrain, of which the first, second, and fourth lines must rhyme. It was epigrammatic: beginning with a reflection or description, it drew a moral in the final line. Witty and intelligent people could express their feelings and opinions. Circulating anonymously and often voicing criticism of imposed doctrines or prohibitions, they were a favorite verse form among intellectuals, who might meet in each other's home and recite a *ruba'i* or two. Persia had for centuries been a wine-drinking culture, but Islam prohibited wine; what could be more natural than to use verses about taverns, the grape, and wine both as descriptors and as metaphors for private opposition to the attempts to stamp out suspicious opinions?

This is what Omar Khayyám did. Everyone knows his most famous one, as translated and remodeled by the Englishman Edward FitzGerald in *The Rubá'iyát of Omar Khayyám* in 1859 and subsequent editions (the standard version of this particular verse is from the fifth edition of 1889):

> *A Book of Verses underneath the Bough,*
> *A Jug of Wine, a Loaf of Bread—and Thou*
> *Beside me singing in the Wilderness—*
> *Oh, Wilderness were Paradise enow!*

This one is harmless enough. But what about this one, which has a touch of anti-Islam about it:

> *And much as Wine has play'd the Infidel,*
> *And robb'd me of my Robe of Honour—well,*
> *I often wonder what the Vintners buy*
> *One half so precious as the Goods they sell.*

This is even clearer in a near-literal translation (not by FitzGerald) of another verse:

> *Drinking wine and consorting with good fellows*
> *Is better than practising the ascetic's hypocrisy;*

If the lover and drunkard are to be among the damned
Then no one will see the face of heaven.

But according to Khayyám, heaven probably does not exist—and this in itself might have been enough to condemn him, had the authorities known:

When the world is filled with the rumour of the fresh rose
Command, love, the wine to be copiously poured;
Don't bother about houris, heavenly mansions,
Paradise, Hell—they're all rumour, too.

For Khayyám, wine was a metaphor for life: drink it while you can, because you will eventually die and there is nothing more:

YESTERDAY *This Day's Madness did prepare;*
TOMORROW's *Silence, Triumph, or Despair:*
Drink! for you know not whence you came, nor why:
Drink! for you know not why you go, nor where.

Yet he was not always so ridden with anguish or such a sense of finality. His *rubá'iyát* must also have struck sparks because of their occasional devil-may-care cynicism:

You know, my Friends, with what a brave Carouse
I made a Second Marriage in my house;
Divorced old barren Reason from my Bed,
And took the Daughter of the Vine to Spouse.

With sentiments like these, and the ability to craft them into memorable verses, it is perhaps no wonder that he, and others like him, recited them to trusted friends while sipping from goblets of wine. Were they the earliest samizdat?

What was the truth about Cleopatra's pearl?

IN ORDER TO impress Mark Antony, Cleopatra supposedly dissolved a fabulously valuable pearl in her cup of wine and drank it. Anyone who has tried this will realize that any wine you might be able to stomach would not be acidic enough to destroy a pearl. Pliny, on the other hand, wrote that "the servants placed in front of her only a single vessel containing vinegar, the strong rough quality of which can melt pearls" (IX.58). This is certainly more plausible, for the acetic acid concentration in vinegar might be sufficient to dissolve a pearl, which is mostly calcium carbonate; however, unless it was crushed first, the process would take rather a long time, and Mark Antony might have lost interest and left. Furthermore, the residual acetic acid would have made the drink distinctly unpleasant. Perhaps she looked into his eyes in a sultry manner in order to distract him while she drank the wine and just swallowed the pearl.

What was Falstaff expecting when he called for more sack?

SACK, OR SACKE, or sherris-sack, or a number of other variations, was a very popular drink from the early Tudor period throughout the next century or so, but it bore only a partial resemblance to the sherry of today. The plays of Shakespeare are littered with references to sack, but probably the most famous, as these things go, is Falstaff's paean in Act IV of *Henry IV, Part II*. He had been challenged for cowardice by Prince John of Lancaster, a son of Henry IV, because "when everything is ended, then you come"—he had managed to miss participating in the crushing of a rebellion. Falstaff denies to Prince John that he is a coward, but he afterward admits to himself that he might be but for sack:

The . . . property of your excellent sherris is the warming of the blood; which before, cold and settled, left the liver white and pale, which is the badge of pusillanimity and cowardice; but the sherris warms it, and makes it course from the inwards to the parts extremes . . . [S]kill in the weapon is nothing without sack, for that sets it a-work.

But sack did more than make men brave: it also

ascends me into the brain; dries me there all the foolish and dull and crudy vapours which environ it; makes it apprehensive, quick, forgetive, full of nimble, fiery, and delectable shapes; which delivered o'er to the voice, the tongue, which is the birth, becomes excellent wit.

So sack was a wine which could make the drinker—depending on the point of view of the spectator—garrulous and foolhardy, or witty and brave.

There is general agreement as to its origins as a Mediterranean wine. The English, who had a centuries-long love affair with the wines of Iberia for reasons of taste and politics—centuries of wars with France had rendered access to claret less than straightforward—were the most notable devotees of sack. In due course, they settled on the sack from southwest Spain. The outcome was general agreement that "sherris-sacke"—and later sherry—could only come from Jerez de la Frontera (as did the name), but in Shakespeare's time and later, sack could also come from the Spanish-dominated Canary Islands. Indeed, in his *Dictionary*, Samuel Johnson defined sack as "a kind of sweet wine, now brought chiefly from the Canaries," adding that "the sack of Shakespeare is believed to be what is now called Sherry."

Sack could be both dry and sweet. Fundamentally, sack was a dry wine, but it could be sweetened by the addition of concentrated juice from a very sweet grape, the Pedro Ximenez (as is the case with sherry today). In Falstaff's day sack was normally sweet, but often the English—who had a notoriously sweet tooth—themselves added sugar or honey to it. It was white or gold or tawny, but never red. It could be harsh and strong, and this wine was often called the sherry sacke, or the sherris-sacke to which Falstaff referred. Bad wine could be doctored by lime, the acid of the wine being neutralized by the alkali, but Falstaff for one forcefully objected to this. In Act II of *Henry IV, Part I*, after calling for a cup of sack, he shouted: "You rogue, there's lime in this sack too! There is nothing but roguery to be found in villainous man; yet a coward is worse than a cup of sack with lime in it"—clearly, to Falstaff a comparison of the utmost contempt. While not precisely a connoisseur, he had his standards.

Sack was the wine of a single year, unlike the sherry of today, which is blended from the wines of a number of years by the solera system. Nowadays the buyer knows what to expect, because sherry producers have house styles; then, it was unpredictable, with wines from the same vintage developing differently in different casks: more or less dry, more or less rich. The conclusion of the writer William Younger was that "Sherry-Sack was Sherry before Sherry became civilized."

Where authorities come to intellectual blows is over the origin of the name *sack*. H. Warner Allen, in his *A History of Wine*, refers sardonically to those English writers who thought that sack was a corruption of *seco*, meaning "dry": their problem was their ignorance of Spanish. His conviction was that it came from the Spanish verb *sacar*, one meaning of which was "to take out commodities from where they were produced to another country: to export." Therefore, wines invoiced as *vinos de saca*, or wines for export, were soon nicknamed *sack*. Younger, in his *Gods, Men, and Wine*, kindly agrees that this argument has a respectable basis, yet is convinced that nevertheless it is wrong. Clearly a practical man, he points out that "sack wine is wine made with a sack," that is, wine made with grape juice strained through a sack, a technique that had been used through the ages; also a scholar, he is careful to buttress his argument with evidence from a contemporary winemaking manual. The only point on which all can agree is that the sack beloved of early modern England bears some resemblance to the sherry of today, but to what extent no one really knows. Also unanswerable is the question, why is sherry now out of fashion and drunk by only a minority?

What did Jane Austen recommend for heartache?

A SPELL living in the heart of Bath would prove enough to rid the most sentimental of Jane Austen devotees of images of gentility, elegance, delicate (though ruthless) intrigue, and the dedicated maintenance of appearances. Now, the city after dark echoes to the cider-fueled roars of matted-haired traveling folk with mangy dogs on strings and corporate discos from the Pump Room, where, in the daylight, one may still take the brackish, ferrous waters and wonder how on earth they ever caught on. The shade of Beau Nash has not walked for many a year, driven out by the allegedly hilarious "Ghost Walk," and by daylight, the glorious honey-colored Regency stonework is almost obliterated by bewildered tourists dodging tat-sellers, tuneless buskers, unicycle specialists, and oddly desolate locals.

But outside the organized Jane Austen walks one can still from time to time encounter what the fanciful might consider the bottled essence of the great novelist, as indeed one of us did: a single, inexplicable, bottle of Klein Constantia in an otherwise depressing low-end bottle shop smelling of cheap cigarettes and damp carpet (a very damp city, Bath). We did not inquire how it got there, to avoid arousing suspicion, but just snapped it up and carried it home, a faint memory stirring in the brain.

Memory did not lie. In chapter thirty of *Sense and Sensibility* Elinor enters the drawing room, having left her sister lying in bed, prostrated by the disappointments of the heart. There she is "joined by Mrs. Jennings, with a wine-glass, full of something, in her hand." How that "something" captures the hopeful anticipation of the wine drinker; no abstainer, Miss Austen, to choose such a precise and evocative word. And the mystery is soon resolved:

> "My dear," said she, entering, "I have just recollected that I have some of the finest old Constantia wine in the house that ever was tasted, so I have brought a glass of it for your sister. My poor husband! how fond he was of it! Whenever he had a touch of his old colicky gout' [see p. 43], he said it did him more good than any thing else in the world. Do take it to your sister."

The notion that what's good for gout is good for heartbreak is pretty counterintuitive, and so it strikes Elinor. Pointing out that her sister Marianne is asleep, she offers to drink the wine herself, reflecting that "though its effects on a colicky gout were, at present, of little importance to her, its healing powers on a disappointed heart might be as reasonably tried on herself as on her sister."

The bottle we found in the unappealing grog shop popped up at a time neither of gout nor heartache, but one could imagine it ameliorating most of life's problems: a honey-colored ambrosia, taken cool (but never cold) from its dark, soothingly eighteenth-century bottle, simultaneously muscular and suave . . . but is it the original? Is this Klein Constantia, this wine of kings and emperors, the same that cheered Jane Austen, that perhaps inspired Frederick the Great to present J. S. Bach with the theme for the *Musical Offering*, that succored Napoleon himself, that Baudelaire in *Les Fleurs du Mal* compared (as he so often compared things) to sex?

Well . . . yes and no. The *terroir* (see p. 15) is the same, overlooking False Bay behind Cape Town, South Africa. But the grapes, and the wines, have seen changes since its foundation in the late seventeenth century. The wine of Constantia, or *vin de Constance*, was brought to its first peak of fame in the late eighteenth century by one Hendrik Cloete; his was a blend of Muscat de Frontignan (aka Muscat Blanc à Petits Grains), red and white Muscatel, Pontac and a touch of Chenin Blanc. On his death in 1818, the land was divided, the higher part becoming Klein Constantia and the lower Groot Constantia. But by the end of the century, it had all gone wrong. Phylloxera (see p. 77) had wreaked havoc in South Africa, as elsewhere, and the show was over. The wine that had soothed kings, emperors, disappointed hearts, and the colicky gout—not Klein Constantia, nor Groot Constantia, but simply Constantia—was no more.

But the whirligig of time brings in its revenges. In 1980, the Klein Constantia estate was bought by Duggie Jooste, who now makes (though in alarmingly small quantities) a new *vin de Constance* from Muscat de Frontignan but minus the other varietals. We have no way of telling what Baudelaire would have thought, but if you listen closely as you draw the cork, it is not too fanciful to imagine the faint echo of Miss Austen's sharp-eyed laughter.

Ceremonial: did you say "Haman" or "Mordecai"?

WINE, as we can frequently see throughout this book, is *the* ceremonial drink—at least in those countries where the grape can flourish. And nowhere more so than in Judaism, where every Sabbath dinner begins with the lighting of the candles, followed by a ritual blessing and sharing of wine, bread, and salt. The *halakha*, or formal Jewish laws, declare that the bread be blessed first, but the honor of reciting the prayer over the wine—the *kiddush*—is considered the greater, which explains a custom that seems odd to non-Jews: the linen cloth that covers the *challah*, or Sabbath bread.

The reason is a good example of the intricacy of human ritual thinking: by being covered, the bread is not officially there on the table. And if it's not there, how can it be blessed? So the head of the household, naturally enough, turns to the next thing on the table—the wine—and recites the *kiddush*. Thus both honor and law are satisfied.

The Jews, like the ancient Greeks, have a tradition of moderation, particularly where wine is concerned. You will seldom see a Jew rise from the Sabbath table—or any other table—the worse for wear, although almost invariably he or she will be *un petit peu élevé*.

Though there is one formal exception: the feast of Purim. This commemorates the story of Esther, who won a beauty contest and married Ahasuerus, King of Persia. Ahasuerus didn't know that Esther was Jewish, and his prime minister, Haman, was a violent anti-Semite who . . . no, let's start with Mordecai, Esther's guardian, who told her to keep quiet about . . . no, let's start with Haman's plans to massacre the Persian Jews, who . . . actually, it all really begins when Esther . . .

No. It's too complex to summarize. Enough to say that Esther persuaded the King, the King sacked Haman and put Mordecai in his place, Mordecai couldn't rescind the ordered massacre but armed the Jews so that they could defend themselves, and the Jews won. Long story short. The Book of Esther contains the whole story, but the relevant point is that not only does the wine flow freely at the feast, but it is also a *mitzvah*—a commandment—for a good Jew to be so drunk on Purim that he or she cannot tell the difference between the words "cursed be Haman" and "blessed be Mordecai."

This, particularly among the more abstemious Hassidim, or

ultra-Orthodox, is more rapidly achieved than more regular drinkers might realize, and Purim in Hassidic areas is more often than not a majestically raucous affair with flailing dancing, fireworks, toy trumpets, tuneless bellowing, singing, and some very quiet and chastened people the following day.

Times being what they are, there have recently been calls—in New York, of course—for zero tolerance of teenage drinking on Purim (remember that a Jew officially becomes an adult at thirteen) and total abstinence (according to the Safe Homes, Safe Shuls, Safe Schools campaign) for those who cannot drink in moderation. Rather splendidly, Rabbi Dr. Tzvi Hersh Weinreb, executive vice president of the Orthodox Union and a clinical psychologist, declares that although the Talmud "clearly states that it is an obligation on Purim" to be too drunk to distinguish between the two phrases, "it is not clear that [it] means to become intoxicated."

One wonders, then, what it *does* mean, and what Esther would have made of it all.

Did Benjamin Franklin really produce a "sprightly claret"?

BENJAMIN FRANKLIN, one of the greatest of the American Founding Fathers, enjoyed drinking wine. He was not the only American colonist who did so, but they all had difficulties getting hold of French wine, generally accounted the best. Great Britain was often at war with France, and during these periods the British government banned the importation of French wine throughout the empire. This meant that it had to be smuggled into the colonies. If the merchant ships carrying the wine managed to evade the Royal Navy, there was still the danger that, after the long voyage, it would be undrinkable. What to do?

Franklin was a realist, and, believing that you had to work with what you had, decided to encourage the making of wine using native American grapes. (Colonists had tried repeatedly to make such wine for the previous century and a half, and, considering the frequently undrinkable result using this raw material, it was advice that betrayed some desperation.) To this end, he printed the necessary instructions in the 1743 edition of his *Poor Richard's Almanack*, repository inter alia of nuggets of folk wisdom such as "Early to bed and early to rise, makes a man healthy, wealthy, and wise," "God helps those who help themselves," "Haste makes waste," "The sleeping fox catches no poultry," "Eat to live, and not live to eat," et cetera, et cetera. His recipe:

Because I would have every Man make Advantage of the Blessings of Providence, and few are acquainted with the Method of making Wine of the Grapes which grow wild in our Woods, I do here present them with a few easy Directions, drawn from some Years Experience, which, if they will follow, they may furnish themselves with a wholesome sprightly Claret, which will keep for several Years, and is not inferior to that which passeth for French Claret [red Bordeaux].

Begin to gather Grapes from the 10th of September (the ripest first) to the last of October, and having clear'd them of Spider webs, and dead Leaves, put them into a large Molasses- or Rum-Hogshead; after having washed it well, and knock'd one Head out, fix it upon the other Head, on a Stand, or Blocks in the Cellar, if you have any, if not, in the warmest Part of the House, about 2 Feet from the Ground; as the Grapes sink, put up more, for 3 or 4 Days; after which, get into the Hogshead bare-leg'd, and tread them down until the Juice works up about your Legs, which will be in less than half an Hour; then get out, and turn the Bottom ones up, and tread them again, a Quarter of an Hour; this will be sufficient to get out the good Juice; more pressing wou'd burst the unripe Fruit, and give it an ill Taste: This done, cover the Hogshead close with a thick Blanket, and if you have no Cellar, and the Weather proves Cold, with two.

In this Manner you must let it take its first Ferment, for 4 or 5 Days it will work furiously; when the Ferment abates, which you will know by its making less Noise, make a spile-hole within six Inches of the Bottom, and twice a Day draw some in a Glass. When it looks as clear as Rock-water, draw it off into a clean, rather than new Cask, proportioning it to the Contents of the Hogshead or Wine Vat; that is, if the Hogshead holds twenty Bushels of Grapes, Stems and all, the Cask must at least, hold 20 Gallons, for they will yield a Gallon per Bushel. Your Juice or Must thus drawn from the Vat, proceed to the second Ferment.

You must reserve in Jugs or Bottles, 1 Gallon or 5 Quarts of the Must to every 20 Gallons you have to work; which you will use according to the following Directions.

Place your Cask, which must be Chock full, with the Bung up, and open twice every Day, Morning and Night; feed your Cask with the reserved Must; two Spoonfuls at a time will suffice, clearing the Bung after you feed it, with your Finger or a Spoon, of the Grape-Stones and other Filth which the Ferment will throw up; you must continue feeding it thus until Christmas, when you may bung it up, and it will be fit for Use or to be rack'd into clean Casks or Bottles, by February.

N.B. Gather the Grapes after the Dew is off, and in all dry Seasons. Let not the Children come at the Must, it will scour them severely. If you make Wine for Sale, or to go beyond the Sea, one quarter Part must be distill'd, and the Brandy put into the three Quarters remaining. One Bushel of Grapes, heap Measure, as you gather them from the Vine, will make at least a Gallon of Wine, if good, five Quarts.

These Directions are not design'd for those who are skill'd in making Wine, but for those who have hitherto had no Acquaintance with that Art.

Franklin's claim that it would not be inferior to "that which passeth for French Claret" can be taken as hype, as an indirect comment on the state of the claret that reached American shores, or as a safe claim by Franklin in that few readers could have made the comparison.

What was George Washington's favorite wine?

THE LOVER of wine in colonial America did not have an easy time of it. France was the hereditary enemy, and Great Britain strove to prevent the import of French wine into the colonies— if available, it had probably been smuggled, and was appropriately costly. Furthermore, even ships carrying wine from European countries friendly to Britain, such as Portugal, had to call into a British harbor to pay tax on it.

George Washington liked wine. Indeed, he tried to grow his own wine grapes at his plantation, Mount Vernon, but the results were discouraging. Native American grapes, which grew in abundance, made distinctly bad wines, while imported vinestock, which made excellent wines, lacked immunity to the native diseases and insects which attacked their leaves and roots. Wine, therefore, had to come from abroad. Washington was a great enthusiast for the one decent wine that was tax-free and thus did not have to be smuggled in, which was madeira. This, in fact, was the only wine widely drunk in the American colonies. Indeed, by the eighteenth century, America was the primary market for madeira, taking one-quarter of the island's production. The reasons were the winds and the ocean waves. In terms of miles, the shortest voyage from Britain to North

America is straight across the Atlantic. But in the days of sail, the longer journey south to catch the trade winds near the Equator and then up the eastern seaboard took the shorter time. On the way, ships invariably called in at Madeira for supplies of food and fresh water and casks of madeira wine. Not only did the wine survive the journey, but it was even improved by it.

A connoisseur of madeira, Washington bought his own casks, storing them at Mount Vernon. Once he became president in 1790, the President's House (after 1814 known as the White House) was stocked by his secretary of state, Thomas Jefferson, with plenty of wine—but, alas for madeira, much of this wine was French, with a particular emphasis on champagne, Château d'Yquem, Frontignan, and Château Lafite. Was it because Washington secretly preferred it? Did his guests expect it? Or was it postnatal defiance of Great Britain?

What color was the "wine-dark sea"?

SOONER OR LATER in every wine lover's life comes the terrible moment when someone raises a glass of wine to the light, peers at it quizzically, and murmurs, in that special tone of voice that people use when they are being deep and poetical, "Ahh . . . the *wine-dark sea.*"

The usual location for this utterance is on the terrace of some benighted Greek taverna overlooking the Aegean, when the owner has just produced something "very special" from the back room with a label made on an inkjet printer that very afternoon. (While the Greeks are keen to bring their wines up to a high international standard, and are frequently succeeding, they are still being undercut in their efforts by tourists who equate Greece with cheap wine and by *tavernistas* who are only too happy to play along.)

The same thing may, indeed, happen in your own home, perhaps over something you brought back from Poros, perhaps over a glass of young and almost black Madiran, pressed from the Tannat grape in southwestern France (or indeed Uruguay, to which it was taken by émigré Basques as a taste of home), a wine that, if you catch it on the wrong foot, comes snarling out of the bottle like some Homeric monster, probably a Cyclops.

But the great question is: what does one *say*? The usual option is to nod and sigh soulfully, but readers of this book are beyond such behavior. You know only too well that the quote is from Homer, and, more specifically, from Andrew Lang's 1883 translation of the *Iliad*. The word that Homer used was *oinos*, which is usually translated as something along the lines of "sunset red." Homer uses it only three times: at sunset after a funeral, during an all-night voyage, and when Odysseus's ship founders in a tempest. But even that is misleading and gets us no further toward working out what color, exactly, the "wine-dark sea" really *was*.

The *Iliad* and the *Odyssey* were set in the Ionian archipelago, around the island of Ithaca (although a recent theory has proposed that Homer's Ithaca was in reality now a peninsula, then an island, on the tip of nearby Cephalonia). Sometimes, when one looks out toward the western Ionian Sea at sunset on a stormy evening, the sea can take on a deep purplish red color not unlike a young Tannat or a taverna's hell-brew. "Aha!" we say to ourselves. "The true, the *wine-dark* sea!"

But we might be wrong. It might just be that *oinos* or "wine-dark" had nothing to do with color at all—or not as we think of it. It wasn't just the sea that Homer called "wine-dark"; it was also sheep. He described Hector's hair as *kyanos*, which seems to be the glinting blue of pottery or lapis lazuli. Honey and nightingales are green—or at least what we'd think of as meaning green. Perhaps his bronze sky isn't so odd, but otherwise

Homer's use of color, and his very restricted color palette, seems distinctly odd to modern eyes.

So the question is, if sheep were the same *oinos* as the sea, did Homer see sheep as wine-colored, or indeed wine as the color of sheep? Was he in some way color-blind? Or—given that other Greek poets such as Pindar and Euripides used the same odd (to us) way of describing color—were they *all* color-blind? They certainly thought about color very differently than we do. According to Theophrastus and Aëtius, the father of Greek color theory, Empedocles, believed that colors were an "effluence" that "moved toward the organ of vision" and that color was "that which fits into the pores of the sense of sight." And these colors could be fitted into four main areas: light (white), dark (black), yellow, and red.

But one thing the last two and a half thousand years of human thought has taught us is that language is a slippery thing, and that words may describe the things we see but also can shape how we see the things we describe. Perhaps the better theory of how the ancient Greeks saw color—these strange people, so much like us yet so utterly different, who described only three colors in the rainbow—is that they weren't talking about the same thing as we are. When Homer described the "wine-dark" sea, perhaps he was talking not about its color but about its *essence*. He was saying not less but *more* than the modern wine critic or the photographer's color meter: something about the essential nature of that sea at that time, which was also true elsewhere of a sheep's coat or of the wine itself, from which the epithet sprang. In the same way that Leonardo da Vinci first noticed and then was enthralled by the similarities between a young woman's flowing hair and the running water of a millstream, so, perhaps, Homer was drawing his attention, and ours, to an underlying connection in nature.

Whatever the truth of it, the next time someone holds that glass speculatively up to the light and that misty look comes into her eyes . . . jump in first and say your piece. Sometimes it's not connoisseurship that counts but gamesmanship.

Who was the first American connoisseur of wine?

THERE IS NO competition here: it was Thomas Jefferson. Not only did he have a great knowledge of wines and a palate to be admired, but he also took steps to ensure that the wine he received was the same as the wine he had bought. Because the new United States needed a minister to France, in 1784, at the age of forty-one, he left the United States for Paris. Here he discovered fine wine. He began to purchase it seriously, and burned to find out more about the best wines. So he became a grand tourist, seeing the sights and drinking the wines, always making detailed tasting notes. Over two years, he traveled through the great wine regions of France, as well as Italy and the Rhine Valley. After tasting dozens of wines, he decided, as quoted by James Gabler, that a white Hermitage from the Rhône Valley was "the first wine in the world without a single exception" (these vineyards now belong to the house of M. Chapoutier and their grapes go to produce Chante-Alouette), but he also bought dozens of bottles of Yquem. He decided that it was best to go directly to the producer to buy his wines: he had discovered that the merchants in Bordeaux and elsewhere blended the wine *after* selling it to the customer, sometimes adding brandy, and therefore the purchaser could never be certain of what he would eventually receive. Furthermore, if it was shipped in cask from the producer to the merchant, there was a real danger that the wagoners would tap it, consuming some of the wine themselves and allowing oxidation of what was left. He decided that the only remedy was for the producer to bottle the wine at the château before it was shipped to him, a practice on which he was to insist. It would be well over a century before this was common practice.

What was Napoleon's favorite wine?

NAPOLEON spent relatively little time thinking about food and drink and scarcely more time consuming it—he was a grabber and a gobbler, and those who were invited to dinner frequently took the precaution of eating at home before dining with the general. Wine was necessary as a beverage, given the doubtful quality of most available water, and on his marches, he appropriated cellars, public and private, in order to provide wine to his troops. As for himself, although he drank a range of wines, he did have preferences. One was champagne, about which he reputedly made a comment that made its way into anthologies about wine: "In victory you deserve champagne, in defeat you need it." It was certainly the case that he bought, and drank, a significant amount, primarily from Jean-Rémy Moët. The two had first met at the military academy at Brienne-le-Château, where Moët had gone to secure orders for his family's champagne. They developed an enduring friendship, and before each of his military campaigns, Napoleon traveled by the Moët estate at Epernay to collect cases of champagne; the lone exception was his dash to Waterloo in 1815, after he had escaped from exile in Elba. His last visit had taken place on March 14, 1814, just before his forces fell to the Allied armies, and it was on this visit that Napoleon pinned on his friend's coat his own Légion d'honneur. This was awarded for his distinguished service to France in increasing the worldwide reputation of its wines.

As for still wines, whenever possible he drank red burgundy, reputedly because he believed that drinking it helped in the conception of male children. His preferences were Clos Vougeot and Chambertin, but, considering that he often drank his wine chilled and diluted with water, it probably mattered little which burgundy was actually in the glass. As do most people, he often drank what was available. His carriage was captured after Waterloo, and it was discovered to contain nearly empty bottles of malaga and rum.

After his defeat at Waterloo, Napoleon was exiled to the very remote Atlantic island of St. Helena from 1815 until his death in 1821. This was more than two thousand miles from the British Cape Colony (now part of South Africa), and over twice that distance from Europe. His household at Longwood House had supplies of champagne, clarets and burgundies, and madeira. Yet what is memorable was the Cape wine Groot Constantia, a fabled sweet white dessert wine drunk by all of the crowned heads of Europe. Napoleon took advantage of his relative proximity to the Cape to indulge his taste for Constantia, 297 gallons of which were shipped in wooden casks from Groot Constantia to St. Helena every year. On his deathbed, he refused everything offered to him save a glass of Constantia wine. Was he first offered champagne but turned it down? If so, the evidence seems to indicate that Constantia was his favorite wine—at the end, at any rate.

What was "the blushful Hippocrene"?

KEATS, in his "Ode to a Nightingale," yearns for

> *a beaker full of the warm South,*
> *Full of the true, the blushful Hippocrene,*
> *With beaded bubbles winking at the brim,*
> *And purple-stainèd mouth,*
> *That I might drink, and leave the world unseen.*

As far as wine writing goes, this is a confused, and confusing, piece of poetry. Hippocrene, for example, has a "true" identity and a Keats-given one. The true identity was that of the spring on Mount Helicon in ancient Boeotia that gushed forth when the foot of the flying horse Pegasus struck the earth. The Muses danced around the spring to find inspiration, and presumably

Keats invoked it because by legend it conferred poetic inspiration on those who drank its waters. But he referred to it as a wine, and here the identity is even more confusing. The poet states that it is a red wine, and that it produces a purple-stainèd mouth. Yet if it is "blushful," that seems to indicate a rosé, which hardly produces a purple mouth. If the beaker has beaded bubbles winking at the brim, it might be a sparkling wine of some sort. Keats, in fact, is calling for a wine that was probably badly made from watery wild grapes and intended to be drunk immediately after the vintage with, perhaps, a bit of fermentation still carrying on. In short, Keats was describing a cheap sparkling red wine—perhaps an ancient red Lambrusco?

What was "the blude-red wine"?

The king sits in Dunfermline town,
Drinking the blude-red wine:
"O whare will I get a skeely skipper
To sail this new ship of mine?"

O up and spake an eldern knight,
Sat at the king's right knee:
"Sir Patrick Spens is the best sailor
That ever saild the sea."

King Alexander III of Scotland had no successor in Scotland, and therefore he gave instructions that his young granddaughter, the Maid of Norway, should be brought back to Scotland. According to Child Ballad number 58, "Sir Patrick Spens," he instructs Sir Patrick to set out immediately, accompanied by a group of Scottish lords, and bring her back. The knight is flattered but very apprehensive, since it is the dead of winter and the sea is treacherous, but he naturally bows to the will of his king. Once in Norway, he falls out with some Norwegian lords, who accuse the Scots of draining away the wealth of the Norwegian king, and in anger Sir Patrick orders the ships to be put ready for departure the following morning. He is warned of the danger of this by one of his sailors:

I saw the new moon late yestreen
Wi' the auld moon in her arm;
And if we gang to sea, master,
I fear we'll come to harm.

And of course, they do: in spite of all attempts by the sailors to save the ship, it goes down.

The ballad ends:

O forty miles off Aberdeen
'Tis fifty fathoms deep,
And there lies gude Sir Patrick Spens,
Wi' the Scots lords at his feet.

The tale told in the ballad, which supposedly took place in 1290, is just that: a tale. However, Alexander's penchant for wine is fully documented: in 1253, for example, he took delivery of a hundred casks. But what wine was it? By the last few decades of the thirteenth century, Scottish merchants were sailing directly to the city of Bordeaux, the capital of Gascony, an English possession since 1152 through the marriage of Henry II to Eleanor of Aquitaine. Scotland and England were not yet mortal enemies—this developed after the death of Alexander—and the Scots sailed out of English ports as well as out of Leith (the port for Edinburgh); they landed in Gascony in safety. The best wine of Gascony came from the upper reaches of the Garonne and Dordogne rivers, primarily from areas near Cahors, Gaillac, and Bergerac, and it was probably this wine that the king drank.

But what was this wine like? It was a thinnish, light-colored, extremely young wine, shipped almost immediately after its fermentation had been completed. Not surprisingly, it was drunk up very quickly lest it turn sour, since by the following summer it would not be worth drinking. Attempts were made to rescue the wine by sweetening it, but although this might change the taste, it did nothing to improve the quality. Calling this wine "blude-red" can only be termed an extreme example of poetic license.

What are the musical grapes of Weingarten?

THERE MAY BE more rarefied topics than the regional economics of medieval and early modern viticulture in what is now Bavaria . . . but none springs immediately to mind. On the one hand, there is the assertion that wine was generally reserved for the landlords and the monastic foundations who actually owned the vines, while the locals made do with beer. On the other hand, there are clear indications that winemaking supported local economies: on the slopes of the Schoenbuch, below the Grafenburg, monks from Ottobeuren had been practicing viticulture since the late twelfth century and the nearby village of Kayh was doing very well—witness the mighty wine press and the prosperous *Rathaus*, or town hall. But when they moved to orchards and cider making in the mid-1600s, their prosperity went on the slide.

But whatever side you take, it seems certain that wine must play a more than trivial role in your economy if you choose to name your community Vineyard—or, in this case, Weingarten, an abbey (and, since 1865, the name of the town) standing on the Martinburg.

Weingarten lies some twelve miles northeast of the Bodensee, the farthest southeasterly outpost of the Baden region. The first surviving records of the name occur in abbey records from 1123, though it had been founded almost a century earlier by Welf IV, count of Schussengau. By the time Frederick Barbarossa was crowned king of Germany at Aachen in 1152, Weingarten's lands—mostly vineyards and forest—stretched from the Allgau to the Bodensee, and the Vineyard Abbey became one of the richest in Germany. In 1715, the great Romanesque basilica was demolished, and a new abbey, built in the Baroque manner, was completed in 1725.

The result is one of the great late flowers of the Baroque, and its biggest surprise comes as the visitor turns to leave. High in the west gallery is one of the most astonishing, beautiful, and magnificently peculiar organs in the world, built by a local cabinetmaker turned organ builder called Joseph Gabler between 1737 and 1750.

It was one of only four organs Gabler completed, and the project was bedeviled with fires, terrible rows about money, and the world's first known Trojan horse (after the original Trojan horse, that is): at one stage, Gabler silenced the entire organ by shutting off a secret valve that nobody else could possibly find in his terrifying maze of wind trunks and pipework, only restoring breath to the instrument when he got paid.

Not being technically entirely adept, Gabler set himself impossible challenges simply because he didn't know they *were* impossible: the organ, though wonderfully sweet-toned, rattled, hissed, and sighed like a living creature, and still does today, even after restoration. At one stage, it was said, Gabler made a pact with the devil: his immortal soul in return for the secret to making a particular stop (the *vox humana,* or "human voice") work effectively; his blood, in which he signed the contract, can still be seen on the pipes. . . .

Yet even in this technical and administrative nightmare, one thing Gabler had no trouble over was the cabinetmaking. The organ soars to the ceiling of the church, winding sinuously around the six vast windows in the west wall. Light floods in over the great four-keyboard console, which looks out over the church; to sit at it is like occupying the pilot's seat on a steampunk jumbo jet.

The whole thing looks as if it should fill the church not with music but with perfume, perhaps of apple and lime, of oil and honey and slate—the strange, disorienting perfumes of Riesling. And, as if in homage, above the console hang vast bunches of grapes. To a more restrained eye, they strike an oddly Dionysian note—quite literally, as it turns out, because as well as the usual (and unusual) pipes of a normal organ, Gabler's haunting fantasy boasts a cuckoo, a nightingale, a drum, and a pedal carillon, and the notes of this carillon are played on *the grapes themselves*, which turn out to be cunningly crafted bells struck with wind-powered hammers.

If Riesling could sing, it would perhaps sing with the voice of Gabler's masterpiece.

Which microorganisms make and mar wine?

LOUIS PASTEUR, who lived from 1822 to 1895, first proved the truth of the "germ theory," which proposes that life-forms too small to be seen by the naked eye are responsible for much natural decay and disease. He is most likely remembered by the general public in the phrase *pasteurized milk*, but it is less well known that he really invented pasteurization for wine; applying it to milk came later. Pasteurization for wine involved holding the liquid, such as the fermented grape must (liquid from pressing the grapes), at just below boiling point for one or two seconds, long enough to kill off the yeasts and stop the fermentation, but not long enough to boil off the alcohol. He was, in fact, the man who first investigated the microbiology of winemaking and wine spoilage, the unsung knowledge vital to successful winemaking.

Winemaking itself depends on controlling a natural process of decay that happens to produce alcohol. Wine grapes have yeasts on their surface, which, if the grapes are crushed and left lying around, cause fermentation (bubbling) and the production of alcohol. This hands-off approach is not a recommended way of producing a drinkable beverage, though surely it must have been the observation of what happened to such damaged grapes that led to the invention of wine. The first microbiological step in proper winemaking involves the *controlled* fermentation of grape must with yeast. In this, the sugars in the grape—glucose and fructose, together sometimes with added cane or beet sugar—are converted into alcohol and carbon dioxide. It is the carbon dioxide that bubbles off. In larger wineries, the yeasts are more likely nowadays to be commercially available, specially selected strains than to be natural yeasts. Having said that, in most small estates in Europe winemakers rely on the long-established natural yeasts that inhabit vineyards and wineries to get the fermentation going. Indeed, many of the greatest wines in a number of countries are made using natural (sometimes called "wild") yeasts.

The next microbiological step in winemaking is malolactic fermentation, used in the making of most red wines and of many white ones. This depends on *Lactobacillus, Leuconostoc,* and/or *Pediococcus* bacteria, and converts malic acid, which is harsh-tasting and found in apples, into less harsh lactic acid and carbon dioxide (which bubbles off).

The main bacterium that mars wine is *Acetobacter*. If this bacterium is present, and also oxygen from the atmosphere, the alcohol is converted into acetic acid (the main ingredient, apart from water, in vinegar) and ethyl acetate (which is what one smells in nail polish remover). Some of these compounds occur in all wines, and indeed, their level may contribute to the overall characteristic of the wine (the famous Lebanese wine Château Musar is an example of this). However, at higher levels, these compounds (known as volatile acidity, or VA) are undeniably a fault.

Modern winemakers take considerable care to exclude oxygen and/or to kill *Acetobacter*.

Finally, one must not forget the fungus that, in the presence of chlorine, acts on cork in such a way as to ruin the bottle of wine on which the cork is used (see p. 86). Bottles of wine destroyed by this microorganism are only too frequently opened by the regular wine drinker.

What is it in port that gives you gout?

CAUSE AND EFFECT are tricky bedfellows, and we are given to getting them wrong, so much so that the commonest error even has its own special Latin tag: *post hoc, ergo propter hoc*—literally "after that, therefore because of that," or in other words, the assumption that because B followed A, A must have *caused* B.

One of the most fascinating examples of *post hoc* involves all those legends about zombies and the Undead and vampires and Nosferatu. What happens, you see, is that . . .

But no. That's not a tale for this book. Another example, though—which certainly *is* in our brief—is the link between wine (especially port) and gout, which just may be wrong, though close.

There are some afflictions that will never be dignified. The pallid figure wasting elegantly on the chaise longue from consumption has a strange glamour. The migraine sufferer, too fraught even to groan in her darkened room, arouses universal sympathy. But contract hemorrhoids, for example, or an ingrown toenail, or a boil on the backside, and you find yourself somehow diminished, an instant object of slapstick fun.

The sufferer from gout is in a similar position. Depictions of him in woodcuts and cartoons show him (for it is invariably a him) seated with a heavily bandaged foot on a cushion; the foot may be depicted as being in flames, gnawed by demons, stabbed with knives, or otherwise tortured. The simplest, and in its way most affecting, example is on the title page of *The Praise of Gout* by Pirckheimer, published in London in 1617: it shows a profoundly saddened man, bandaged foot on a footstool, stick in hand, being examined by a tall-hatted physician, one hand raised in admonition, the other palpating the gouty leg. From the patient's mouth issues a speech scroll. He is uttering one word and one word only: "Oh."

You can see the picture, and many others, in Porter and Rousseau's *Gout: The Patrician Malady*. For a disease—or, rather, a *symptom*—to get a book all to itself argues some distinction, and indeed the roll of gout sufferers in history is as distinguished as it gets. Science writer John Emsley lists some of the known sufferers: Benjamin Franklin, William Pitt, Tennyson, Charles Darwin, and, curiously for an ailment associated with intemperance, John Wesley, the founder of Methodism. Suspected sufferers include Alexander the Great, Kublai Khan, Christopher Columbus, Martin Luther, and Isaac Newton. It was no respecter of classes, either, despite its reputation as "the patrician malady": while the port drinkers of the eighteenth century suffered from "saturnine gout," it also afflicted moonshine drinkers in the twentieth-century United States. Outbreaks of gout were common, often named after where they started: seventeenth-century France was hit by the Picton colic, and the eighteenth century saw the Massachusetts dry gripes. Nor is it even a modern affliction: Roman writers Seneca, Ovid, and Virgil and the vicious satirist Juvenal all poked fun at the gouty, Juvenal suggesting that the famous athlete Ladas "wouldn't hesitate to take on the rich man's gout, for there's not much to be got out of running fast."

But it's in the writings of the first-century encyclopedist Pliny (see p. 100) that we get our first clue as to what might be *really* going on. Pliny was a man who knew his wines, and Robert Harris, in his novel *Pompeii*, has him plausibly first noticing the beginning of the Vesuvius eruption in the ripples in a glass of Caecuban wine, "forty years old and still drinking beautifully."

Pliny describes the process of making *sapa*, used as a sweetener for wine or drunk neat: "The wine known as 'sapa' is grape must, boiled down until only a third is left; it's sweeter made from white must."

And there is the clue: the *sapa* was boiled down in pans with a high lead content. Could it be that lead was somehow responsible for the gout?

Gout itself is an agonizing inflammation caused by uric acid crystals, like sharp needles, lodging themselves in the joints, particularly of the feet and ankles as gravity does its work. Normally, uric acid is excreted by the kidneys, but lead interferes with the process and the acid crystals build up. So certainly lead is a candidate.

But is it the common link? In the eighteenth century, the port wine so popular in England (and out of the reach of the ordinary man's pocket) was already contaminated with lead salts: lead oxide dissolved in wine vinegar was used to adulterate wine, both to sweeten it and to kill extraneous yeasts that might spoil the fermentation.

Worse, port—and indeed madeira—were both wines that would keep once opened, and kept they were, in decanters made from crystal that could contain up to 32 percent lead. The lead could, and did, leach from the glass decanters into the wine: after four months, the wine could contain up to 5 ppm of lead, up to 70 percent of which would be absorbed into the body.

This may explain the habit of the time of "taking the waters" at spas such as Bath. The constant water drinking would have increased the flow of urine and washed out, literally, some of the excess lead, allowing the uric acid to be redissolved and alleviating the agonizing symptoms.

And the moonshine drinkers of Kentucky? Their homebrew was often distilled using automobile radiators as condensers; the radiators were held together with lead solder, which, once again, leached into the liquor.

So, yes, port *would* cause gout—but not by direct cause and effect. The malady was not itself a sort of moral punishment for boozy libertinism, but partly a result of scientific ignorance and partly a side effect of port's good keeping qualities, which allowed it to lie in decanters and absorb more lead. *Post hoc ergo propter hoc?* Yes—but only partly.

Why is white burgundy so risky?

WHITE BURGUNDY, made from the Chardonnay grape and aged in oak, can be remarkably delicious, sometimes sublime, and frequently expensive. But it is horribly prone to oxidation, which takes place when the wine is damaged by the small amounts of oxygen that pass through the cork during storage. You can usually tell just by looking that the wine is oxidized, because over the years the color darkens from a light yellow to a much darker shade, continues to amber, and ends up brown. You can also tell by sniffing it, because it often has the aroma of madeira—hence the alternative term *maderized*. It does not, however, taste like madeira; it tastes foul.

White burgundies from the 1995 to 1999 vintages became notorious for not keeping and improving as their purchasers had expected. On being opened in the early 2000s, when they should have been drinking well, they were found to be maderized. A particularly plausible explanation is that not enough sulfur dioxide had been put into the wine at bottling. Winemakers try to protect the flavor of the wine by adding a small amount of sulfur dioxide, recognizable by the acrid smell of burning matches. In the early 1990s, however, critics complained that the smell of sulfur dioxide was too strong, and consequently many winemakers in Burgundy cut back on the amounts they used. Whether or not this is the correct explanation (there are other theories), such was the dismay and outrage—for these were expensive wines—that Web sites were set up to exchange horror stories. Whatever the causes, huge numbers of bottles were found to be maderized, and whole cases of wine were poured down the sink.

Why do we drink red wine too hot?

YOU ARE TIRED and hungry after a long, hot, sunny day, and you have decided to go to your local Italian restaurant for some comfort food, such as lasagne or ravioli. In spite of the open windows, the restaurant is hot from all of the people and the continual cooking. You order some of the restaurant's decent and reasonably priced red wine to go with their excellent food. The bottle is opened, but the wine is warm, and it tastes rather limp. You boldly ask the waiter for a bucket of water and ice, and partially submerge the bottle in it. After ten minutes, you find that the wine has cooled nicely and now tastes as you expected.

Hugh Johnson, in the inside cover of his annual *Pocket Wine Book,* has a chart of recommended drinking temperatures. The range for red wines is from 11°C for Beaujolais (for an approximate Fahrenheit equivalent double the centigrade and add 30, so 11°C is 52°F) to 64°F for the best red Bordeaux and other top reds. For "standard daily reds," he recommends 55–57°F. The Italian restaurant stores the wine on shelves that can be seen by the diners, and thus your bottle has reached a temperature of, say, 81°F: the wisdom of the ice bucket is confirmed.

Go back a hundred years and imagine that it is wintertime. Some wine-drinking gentlefolk have the butler bring up a bottle of their best claret from the cellar, which has a temperature of about 50°F. They may be well off, but keeping their high-ceilinged dining room much above 64°F is well nigh impossible.

Consequently, they have the bottle opened and left in the dining room for several hours to allow it to warm to the right temperature. In the summer, when the dining room is rather warmer and the cellar may be at 59°F, they will not have to wait as long before the wine is at the perfect temperature—that is, winter room temperature—to be best appreciated.

Nowadays, most wine drinkers lack both cellar and servant, but they do have central heating. Winter or summer, if they leave the wine around the house or, worst of all, just keep it in the kitchen, they will regularly be drinking red wine at a temperature that unbalances the flavors. The idea that wine ought to be drunk at room temperature or *chambré* is no longer a good one. Room temperature has outpaced the traditional advice, and too many wine drinkers fail to store the wine in a cool environment in the first place.

So, in the absence of any cool storage for your red wine, you need to do the opposite of what the gentlefolk of 1908 did, which is to cool it. If you haven't got any ice handy, you can use the refrigerator: it is not as fast as the bucket of water and ice, but it works. Your fridge is at about 44°F, and it takes about one hour and forty-five minutes for a bottle of wine to split the difference of temperature when moved from one place to another (this conclusion is the result of original research first revealed here). So if the house is at 70°F and you are drinking a "standard daily red," one hour and forty-five minutes in the fridge will bring it to the correct temperature (57°F) for pleasurable drinking.

Why do we drink white burgundy too cold?

LET's SAY that you've decided to have a roast chicken for dinner, but you're not in the mood for a good claret; you settle on a nice white burgundy or California chardonnay instead. A few minutes before you take the chicken out of the oven, you take the burgundy out of the fridge. It is delicious, and goes very well with the chicken. After dinner, you cork the bottle and leave it on the table, intending to return it to the fridge before going to bed. However, at that point, you decide to pour yourself another glass. To your delight, it is even better: as it has warmed up, it has developed, and aromas and flavors you had failed to notice before now suffuse your nose and mouth.

Most people drink white burgundy too cold because they probably haven't noted the advice of the great and good wine experts, and even if they have, it's just as difficult in a modern environment to avoid drinking white burgundy too cold as to avoid drinking red wine too hot. The British wine writers Oz Clarke, Hugh Johnson, and Jancis Robinson all agree that a complex wine such as a white burgundy should be drunk much warmer than other white wines. Johnson's recommendation is 57 to 59°F, actually a little warmer than his recommendation for "standard daily reds."

Most people don't have cellars, so they tend to keep white wines in the refrigerator. For most whites the temperature of the refrigerator (44°F) is closer to the best drinking temperature than is the temperature of the house—but for white burgundy or most reds, neither the refrigerator nor the house is much good. The temperature of a modern house is probably 70°F in the winter, thanks to central heating, and hotter in the kitchen and in the summer. If the house is indeed at 70°F and the refrigerator at 44°F, then keep the burgundy in the refrigerator, taking it out and leaving it out in the house for about one hour and forty-five minutes before drinking it; alternatively, leave it in the house and put it in the refrigerator for the same amount of time. Either way, the wine will have got to about 57°F. And in a restaurant, don't leave the white burgundy in the ice bucket for too long.

Alas, getting the temperature right won't help if the white burgundy is oxidized (see p. 46). But if it is in good condition and also served at the right temperature, bliss.

What does the Six-Day War have to do with wine?

WHAT A CAPRICIOUS lot we are; how quickly fashions change. A little over a hundred years after Cicero's comment (see p. 60) suggesting that old wines tend to go sour, along comes the Gospel of Luke, declaring (in chapter 5, verse 39) that "no man having drunk old wine immediately desireth new: for he saith, The old is better."

Of course, we don't know what the author of Luke meant by "old" and "new" wine. What we *do* know is that viticulture was known in Palestine, Judea, or Israel (or whatever the land was called at any particular time) at least a thousand, and possibly two thousand, years before Luke: the Book of Deuteronomy (chapter 8, verse 8) specifically praises the vine, and the Song of Solomon begins with an erotic linking of love and wine: "Let him kiss me with the kisses of his mouth: for thy love is better than wine." And Noah got drunk on wine, which led to a *lot* of trouble.

But in modern times, the wines of Israel have had—at least from the wine lover's point of view—a patchy time of it, not least because of the Jewish dietary laws. The principles of *kashrut*, which set out which foods are forbidden because they are "unclean" (the rules derive mainly from the Book of Leviticus and serve as the laws of the Temple priests, described by one rabbi of our acquaintance as "instructions for the greatest barbecue in the history of civilization"), would at first sight not seem to apply to wine. But what anthropologists are keen on calling "foodways" are intricate and fundamental to a culture. In the old triad: "I eat normally, you are picky, they are fanatics."

Wherever you stand on *kashrut,* the rules are, to say the least, interesting. Wine cannot be kosher if it might have been "poured out to an idol." Wine that has been boiled cannot be used for idolatry, so it remains kosher even if it has been touched by an "idolator." Wine cannot be kosher if it has been touched by someone who believes in idolatry, or if it has been produced by Gentiles. And there are a number of prohibitions about "mingling"—nothing really to do with wine, but designed to prevent Jews and non-Jews mixing together in, shall we say, too relaxed a fashion, which might lead to intermarriage.

All this is taken very seriously by *frum*—highly devout, Orthodox—Jews. And it might be said not to have had the best effect on Israeli winemaking. For a start, the *mevushal*, or boiled, wines really never stood a chance. Cooking the wine ruins it, as anyone who has tried microwaving a bottle and overshot the mark will have discovered. The result is thin, feeble, purplish stuff not really fit for drinking. Some winemakers now use flash pasteurization and assert that this does not harm the wines and may even improve them, but the main reason for doing it is so that your Catholic waiter can draw the cork and pour your wine without it ceasing to be kosher.

The supply of kosher wines was for many years effectively monopolized by the Israeli drinks giant Carmel. As *New York Times* wine writer Howard G. Goldberg put it: "Its merchandising in the American-Jewish market had long coasted on a mishmash of Zionism, economic and political and social support for Israel, sentimentality, generations of brand familiarity, Passover seder requirements and similarity to sweet Manischewitz. Quality? Forget it."

But the Six-Day War in 1967, which resulted in Israel capturing the Golan Heights, and the Yom Kippur War of 1973, which secured its position, marked a change in Israeli winemaking, which moved, figuratively and literally, upward. The Heights proved perfect for viticulture, and the modern Israeli wines started to appear. Now, with the expertise of winemakers who learned their craft in France, Australia, and the United States, the Heights are producing some international-class wines, and the Galil Mountain winery, for example, is producing over a million bottles a year.

Foodways, religions, wars, and wine: once again, we see at least a glimpse of the unexpected interconnectedness of things.

"Wine diamonds": what are they, and are they dangerous?

IN THE OLDEN DAYS, say forty years ago, most white-wine drinkers expected to find crystals left as a deposit in wine. These crystals (usually potassium hydrogen tartrate) mostly stick to the glass and thus are not swallowed; even if they were swallowed, it would not matter in the least, because they are harmless, if a bit crunchy. However, younger wine drinkers can, naturally, fear that their presence is a fault in the wine. Indeed, many producers nowadays go to considerable lengths, possibly losing quality in other respects, to avoid crystals. Those who do not try to avoid crystals instead have renamed them: as one German label reads, "This wine contains Wine Diamonds, which are an entirely natural deposit." Another highly respected German producer is more blunt: "*Mit zunehmender Flaschenreife kann Weinstein ausgeschieden werden. Es sind Salze der Weinsäure, die in keiner Weise den Geschmack beeinträchtigen. Ein Grund zur Reklamation bzw. Rückgabe des Weines ist somit nicht gegeben.*" In English: "With increasing bottle age, potassium hydrogen tartrate can separate out . . . [which] in no way impairs the taste. This is no reason for complaining or expecting your money back."

What links Papuan pigs, peacocks, and Pétrus?

THERE IS ALWAYS a *vin du jour*, just as there is always a *plat du jour*, the difference being that the former is most clearly distinguished by its price. Currently, it's Pétrus: unarguably one of the great Pomerols, it has nevertheless acquired a bit of a name for itself as the choice of the sort of people we hate in restaurants (unless we are restaurateurs, in which case they are the sort of people we love).

The stories come round regularly of slicked-back roaring derivatives traders running up five-figure bills as they knock back the stuff at $10,000 a bottle, bellowing with excitement and hubris as they try to outdo each other. Unlike some Chinese newcomers (see p. 153) to the Bordeaux *grands crus*, these young men (for so they usually are—time travelers from the 1987 film *Wall Street* in attitude if not in dress) seldom if ever soften the edges with a measure of Sprite or Coca-Cola. But all the same, in the majority of cases it's fair to say that the people at that table over there who are ruining your evening aren't drinking Pétrus. They aren't even drinking wine.

They are drinking money.

The whole purpose of the process is to display their excess of wealth. It's an evolutionary strategy for reproduction that finds its corollary in the peacock's tail: an unnecessary and, frankly, burdensome piece of flashiness that exists purely as a declaration that the owner can afford it.

The traders might also be surprised to learn that they are reenacting a timeless ritual that elsewhere is performed with pigs. In the Moka ceremonies of Papua New Guinea, the "big men" vie for status and power by making, and receiving, gifts of ever finer and fatter pigs. The same principle is at work in the Kula and Sepic Coast exchanges of Papua New Guinea and, perhaps most famous, the potlatch ceremonies of many Pacific Northwest tribes, including, most euphoniously, the Nuu-chah-nulth and the Kwakwaka'wakw, although the word *potlach* itself comes from the Chinook.

The crucial thing about potlatch is that status is determined not by what you have but by what you give away. And even though missionaries tried to stop the Native Americans from holding potlatch ceremonies (which were apparently the biggest impediment to making decent Christians out of peoples who regarded themselves as perfectly decent anyway), the practice, once you get your eye in, can be seen all over the world in some strange guises. Admire a Gulf princeling's wristwatch and he will give it to you. Admire a man's wife in an "alternative lifestyle" community—Cap d'Agde in southwestern France, so they say, or those strange conventions that tend to pop up in Las Vegas—and he will invite you to take her upstairs. Stories abound of tribes (usually unspecified) among whom potlatch is taken even further: admire, say, an intricate, priceless ancestral carpet and the owner will shrug, murmur, "What, this old thing?" roll it up, and hurl it on the fire, which presumably is kept blazing for just such an occasion.

In the West, though, we are more circumspect. Gifts of great value tend to be given only to those from whom the giver has at least a sporting chance of getting them back. And a Russian oligarch whose wife is weighed down with glittering jewelry might be said not to be practicing potlatch at all: he is not distributing his wealth but displaying it. There's all the difference in the world.

But when it comes to things that are by their very nature evanescent—who would drink that $10,000 Pétrus two days after the cork was drawn?—Western culture is more liberal in its potlatch ceremonials. To give your guests a fine claret or a perfect Yquem is considered a compliment to them, and a reflection of the host's standing. There is still the problem of price—what if your guests don't know how much that bottle of La Tâche cost you?—and so those who are anxious that the full ceremonies be observed do so either outside the home, in a restaurant where everyone can see the wine list (or at least the bill), or with something whose price is all too well known.

And it is this position that Pétrus occupies. There can be few, even the dedicated beer drinker with the palate of a vulture,

who do not know that Pétrus is very pricey, and forms an opin-
ion of their host accordingly.

Not that it always works: a cartoon in *Punch* by the late
Michael ffolkes showed a peacock in full glorious display saying
bemusedly to a drab and unimpressed peahen: "What do you
mean, 'no'?"

Particularly now that the more raucous Pétrus
drinkers have been shown up as the very people
who have, temporarily at least, brought the
United States and satellite economies into
the mire, we might suspect that, as with pea-
cocks, so with men. . . .

Is the new Beaujolais in yet?

IN 1977 Mike Leigh's brilliant play *Abigail's Party* presaged the
British wholehearted embracing of upward mobility and con-
spicuous aspirational materialism. And wine, of course, played
its part. Even more than thirty years on, the unspeakable Beverly (played in the original TV production by Alison Steadman,
who managed to look like a frantic trucker in drag) continues to
arouse knowing and derisive laughter from the posh part of the
audience when, given a bottle of wine by the frozen, thrifty
Ange, she looks at the label, cries, "Ooo, nice, Beaujolais, I'll
just pop it in the fridge, okay?"

How we laugh. Red wine? *In the fridge?* Honestly. These people.
How embarrassing.

Beaujolais itself was, in the late 1970s, a little suspicious. In
1972 a *Sunday Times* journalist, Allan Hall, had issued a challenge to readers. The idea of the Beaujolais nouveau (or *primeur*)
was originally a sort of local knees-up to mark the end of the harvest and to drink the *vin de l'année,* the first of the new wine. It
was decided in 1938 that the new wine could only be *sold* after

December 15, but the restrictions were countermanded by the Beaujolais growers' union, the UIVB (Union Interprofessionelle des vins du Beaujolais), in 1951, who cannily put a formal date on the release of the new wine (which, since 1985, has been fixed as the third Thursday in November), so making it a special occasion of sorts.

Allan Hall's challenge was simple: who could be the first to bring back bottles of the nouveau to Britain?

He wasn't the first to have the idea—that slightly dubious honor must go to Georges Duboeuf, the *négociant*, who had established the idea of a race to Paris with the new wine—but Hall brought it to Britain, where it was enthusiastically taken up, despite the fact that nine times out of ten the *vin de l'année* was not really worth drinking. People competed in cars, on trains and motorcycles, and by light aircraft and helicopter, and every wine bar worth its salt was hung with tricolor bunting and the phrase *"Le Beaujolais nouveau est arrivé!"* By the 1990s, the Beaujolais race had spread across Europe, to America and into Asia, and in due course the American market had its way and the slogan changed to "It's Beaujolais Nouveau Time!"

All very clever—particularly for the American industry, which heavily promoted the wine for Thanksgiving, which, by luck or by providence, falls precisely a week later.

So all in all, the sales of Beaujolais rose and the reputation of Beaujolais fell.

But times change and tastes change and, back at *Abigail's Party*, the hoots of laughter at her gaffe about the fridge now inspire superior smiles from the even posher part of the audience who regard themselves as the *real* cognoscenti. For the fashion now—and with a young Beaujolais, fruity and low in tannin, it's a thoroughly good fashion for once—is to drink it lightly chilled.

As a footnote, at one point in the play the terrible Ange suggests, as a "very economical" dish, sardine curry. It's not an idea to dwell on, but when we wonder what goes nicely with a curry (see p. 150) we might indulge in some 1970s nostalgia and imagine a plate of curried canned sardines with a nice new Beaujolais straight from the fridge.

Or not.

A glass of cryogenic wine, anyone?

LET'S SAY you're in Germany on business and you want to impress your colleagues with your familiarity with a wine list as well as with the depth of your pockets. Order a bottle of Eiswein. It is unbelievably sweet—some Germans put a drop or two of cognac on the top just to cut the sweetness, which seems somehow to miss the point—and stunningly expensive. Eiswein—literally, "ice wine"—is made from grapes that have frozen as hard as marbles in temperatures of at least 18°F. In Germany, on the first November or December day when this temperature is reached, pickers stumble out into the dark and, between 5 A.M. and 8 A.M., pick the grapes, which are then taken straight to the winery and pressed. The water has frozen out as pure ice, so the acidity, sugar, and flavors are concentrated in the remaining liquid. When the juice runs, the ice crystals are left behind in the press. Riesling Eiswein, a mouthful of which is a celebration of fragrant sweetness and racy acidity, commands a phenomenal price.

But Germany is not the only country that has both grapes and frost. Strong competition for Eiswein comes from Canadian Icewine. Canada has a real advantage over Germany. German winemakers are not guaranteed such cold weather, while in Ontario, 18°F in winter is normal. The Canadians wrap themselves up in parkas and fur hats, head out to the vineyards, and pick the grapes while kneeling in the snow. Because winter in Canada is pretty predictable, the cost of Icewine is rather less than that of Eiswein. This matters, but it is also the case that, although the mode of making the two wines is similar, the results are very different. While Eiswein is sweetness with a streak of acidity, Icewine, with higher sugar levels at harvest time, is higher in alcohol and a marvel of opulent, honeyed sweetness.

Of course, what you are really paying for is rarity. In Canada, the right natural conditions are more common than in Germany. However, a freezer operating at the right temperature will achieve exactly the same effect. So there is another choice: the use of cryoextraction to artificially produce the same type of wine—though not with the same rarity. Freshly picked grapes are frozen overnight in a special cold room and then pressed immediately. (The colder the room, the more concentrated the juice, but the smaller the volume. Therefore, the winemaker can create what he wants at the retail price he wants.) In England, where the right *natural* conditions are hardly ever likely to prevail, one winemaker uses freezing to produce what he calls "cryogenic wine." Since the early 1980s this technique has been used increasingly in Sauternes, even by the most notable producers. The 1987 weather in Sauternes was so wet that many estates marketed no wine at all; those who did may have saved their wine by a little freezing. You could be tempted to look on a bottle of 1987 Sauternes with a speculative eye.

Ceremonials: why did Alcibiades arrive drunk?

FOR ONE OF THE foundation stories of Western thinking, Plato's *Symposium* begins in an alarmingly confusing way. Written around 385 BC, it tells the story of a dinner party and, more important, of a long discussion by the guests on that most enduring of topics, the nature of love. But it is not narrated by Plato himself: the story is told by one Apollodorus (literally, "God's gift"), yet even he doesn't tell it straight. Apollodorus tells us that he was asked about this party "the day before yesterday" by one

Glaucon, who thought it had just happened. "Not at all," says Apollodorus; "it was when we were children, and I was told about it by Aristodemus, who said he was there, and I asked Socrates about it, too, and he agreed with what Aristodemus said, so since I already told Glaucon about it, now I'll tell you . . ."

There can be few more irritatingly oblique ways of starting a story, and one might suspect that, before sitting down to write, Plato himself had been at the Chian. But he pretty soon gets a grip on himself and begins his tale.

The discussions of love run smoothly enough until, well into the party, their debate is interrupted by a roaring and shouting in the courtyard. It is the rugged and heroic Alcibiades, reputedly the most handsome man in Athens (and with whom Socrates is madly in love; this was classical Greece, after all), who has arrived with a (euphemistically named) flute girl and a group of friends. They are all pickled. Alcibiades can barely walk and is wreathed in ivy, violets, and ribbons. Announcing himself as "drunk, utterly sozzled," Alcibiades is invited in, settles down next to Socrates (with whom he exchanges insults and suggestive and slightly arch promises), and demands more drink. Everyone else is still sober, he declares, and that's not fair. "Until you are in adequate drinking order," he says, "I appoint myself as *symposiarch*." He calls for a big cup, then changes his mind and demands the wine cooler, which holds more than half a gallon, and drains it dry. Then he tells them to fill it up for Socrates, "not that it will have any effect on him. He can drink any amount without getting drunk."

This all unpacks rather nicely. Given what we think we know about the ancient Greek symposium—literally, a "drinking party"—we might assume that any not entirely sober-minded person would take care to build up a head of steam before arriving. The proceedings seem, initially at least, pretty strait-laced, verging on the stupefyingly dull. Like so many aspects of life in ancient Athens, the drinking party was, theoretically at least, as highly ritualized and rigidly organized as any Rotary Club dinner.

We know a reasonable amount about what they actually drank. They preferred a degree of sweetness in their wine but didn't attach so much value to its age (perhaps because of cellaring problems; a few hundred years later, the Roman Cicero wrote that "just like wine, so not all men turn sour with old age," suggesting that an old wine was not necessarily a good wine). The best wines were said to come from the islands, especially Chios, Thasos, Lesbos, and Cos. Chian wine could be dry, medium, or sweet, but it was generally white and light-bodied, and much favored in Athens. It might or might not be resinated, and it could be very expensive. Thasian wine was noted for its fragrance, with a hint of apples. It was usually red or even black; in Thasos itself it might be sweetened with honey. Coan was white and strongly flavored with seawater; Lesbian wine also had a flavor of the sea but was not mixed with seawater. Some of it was on the light side, but Lesbos also produced one of the greatest wines of the Greek world, Pramnian. This was rather like Tokaji Essence today, made from the syrup oozing from the grapes under their own weight, before the grapes were pressed.

To choose the wine, a *symposiarch*, or master of ceremonies, was appointed in advance. The symposiarch decided what wine would be drunk (Thasian, Chian, Lesbian, or whatever suited his taste), to what degree it would be diluted with water, and whether that water would be fresh or seawater, a very strange idea to our tastes. He would also decide upon the topic of conversation, and who would speak when. Imagine listening to a man in a beard explaining that tonight "we shall consume a rather, em, *agreeable* wine from the Isle of Cos, diluted in, um, a ratio of, I suggest, er, two parts seawater, three parts freshwater, and two parts of wine, except for the after-dinner libation to Agathos Daimon, of course, ha ha. Then the conversation will be upon, ahem, *sex* . . . ."

And after that there would be the songs, and then the flute girls, and the *hetaerae* (a sort of courtesan-cum-geisha). It is all too easy to imagine the weary guest thinking, "Merciful heavens, do we *have* to have the flute girls . . . ?"

One way of dealing with it was, as Alcibiades worked out, to stoke up before you arrived. But the ritual and particularly the dilution of the wine (the libation was the only point where neat wine passed the lips) were all part of the Athenians' golden rule that the worst thing a man could do was *lose control*. Remaining in command was the vital thing for these people: in command of the body, in command of the thoughts, in command of one's speech, in command—as much as was compatible with the caprices of the gods—of one's destiny (though not, perhaps, quite as much in command of one's household as one might wish, as witnessed by many Greek comedies, above all the *Lysistrata* of Aristophanes, in which the women go on a sex strike until their husbands agree to stop waging war all the time).

In particular, the Greeks disliked Mothon, the goblin-spirit of drunkenness (and bestiality), and believed that only barbarians— like the Scythians and Thracians—drank their wine neat. Hence the dilution of the wine. Even half-and-half with water was considered risky, and the preferred dilution was five parts water to two parts wine. As we all know, it's perfectly possible to get drunk on watered wine; you simply have to drink more. But dilution certainly shows the *intention* of controlling one's drinking, and hence oneself.

Yet it was not infallible. James Davidson, in his scholarly and wonderfully entertaining study of the ancient Greeks' appetites, *Courtesans and Fishcakes,* recounts "a bizarre story told by Timaeus of Taormina" (now a popular Sicilian tourist resort: "Book your Charme Accommodation and enjoy the Sun of Taormina!" announces the Web site) that "illustrates graphically the sense of separation between the world within and the world without the drinking-party":

In Agrigentum there is a house called "the trireme" for the following reason. Some young men were getting drunk in it, and became feverish with intoxication, off their heads to such an extent that they supposed they were in a trireme, sailing through a dangerous tempest; they became so befuddled as to throw all the furniture and fittings out of the house as though at sea, thinking that the pilot had told them to lighten the ship because of the storm. A great many people, meanwhile, were gathering at the scene and started to carry off the discarded property, but even then the youths did not pause from their lunacy. On the following day, the generals turned up at the house, and charges were brought against them. Still sea-sick, they answered to the officials' questioning that in their anxiety over the storm they had been compelled to jettison their superfluous cargo by throwing it into the sea.

"Still sea-sick" is rather splendid, but the most telling words are these: *young men*. As generation after generation has found out in the two and a half thousand years since, you can regulate, ritualize, formalize, and even legislate as much as you like. (For the ancient Greeks—as for most of Europe now—eighteen was the age at which Plato suggested you could start to drink. Unlike most of Europe now, he also said that once you were over forty, and therefore *old*, you could summon up Dionysos and go for it.) But then, as now, throw young men into the mix, and it can all go quickly overboard.

Did the 1855 Bordeaux classification have anything to do with quality?

THIS HANDY setting-out in categories of the so-called best wines of the left bank of the rivers Gironde and Garonne has an apparently unbreakable hold on the throat of the wine trade and of the more affluent consumer. It must be said at the outset that any relationship between this classification and quality was indirect. In 1855, Prince Napoléon-Jérôme, organizer of the Emperor Napoleon III's 1855 Exposition Universelle in Paris, asked the Bordeaux Chamber of Commerce for a comprehensive exhibition of the wines of the Gironde, to be arranged by category. It was based on the red wines of the Médoc and on the sweet white wines of Sauternes-Barsac. St. Emilion's classification had to wait until 1955 and that of the Graves until 1953 (reds) and 1959 (whites), while Pomerol still awaits its equivalent measured consideration.

The task was eagerly undertaken by brokers (*courtiers*), who were considerably more interested in the commercial possibilities arising from the exhibition than in anything else, although they were also keen to impose some order on a chaotic market. Their approach was, first, to list sixty of the leading châteaux of the Médoc plus the great wine of the Graves, Haut-Brion, categorizing them as *premiers*, *deuxièmes*, *troisièmes*, *quatrièmes*, and *cinquièmes crus* (growths), and, second, to list the best sweet white wines of Sauternes and Barsac in two categories, *premiers* and *deuxièmes crus*, with Château d'Yquem on a pinnacle of its own as *premier cru supérieur*. But they did nothing so unnecessary as to taste the wines in order to put each in its rightful place. Rather, they listed the wines in descending order according to the prices they fetched in the market, assuming that the prices reflected the relative quality of the wines. There had been earlier classifications of quality, a rough one in 1647 and another in 1767, and these provided a context. They also paid some attention to lists compiled by well-known connoisseurs such as Thomas Jefferson (see p. 34) and the respectively English and Scottish connoisseurs and writers Cyrus Redding and Dr. Alexander Henderson. The list was then issued through the Chamber of Commerce.

The list is undeniably useful to wine merchants and for those wine buyers unable to taste before buying—that is, most of them—but it has significant flaws. First of all, it seems to be virtually immutable, with only one new entrant into the classification of *premier cru*, Mouton-Rothschild in 1973. This also means that châteaux whose quality demands that they should be elevated to a higher classification, those whose depressing level of quality should cause them to be thrown out, and those wines classified *cru bourgeois* whose quality should admit them to the system are frozen in the positions they held when the dance ended in 1855. Second, the wines around Margaux were the focus of the brokers, while those situated further north, particularly those around St. Estèphe, were largely disregarded. This was overwhelmingly because the lack of a railway to the northern Médoc meant that transport costs to the city of Bordeaux were high. And third, the mergers, acquisitions, and breakups affecting virtually all of the estates over the past century and a half mean that the fundamental basis of the classification—that of a wine produced from the grapes grown on land belonging to a named estate—is, at the least, muddied. The whole situation supports the theory that the human quest for certainty is stronger than the desire for a more truthful ambiguity.

Have some madeira, m'dear?

> She was young, she was pure, she was new, she was nice
> She was fair, she was sweet seventeen
> He was old, he was vile, and no stranger to vice
> He was base, he was bad, he was mean

So begins Flanders and Swann's great hymn to the evil seducer, which manages to entangle the innocent madeira in its toils, and not since Clarence drowned in his malmsey butt has this harmless and indeed benevolent drink taken such a blow to its reputation. The innocent escapes in the end, but not before:

Unaware of the wiles of the snake-in-the-grass
And the fate of the maiden who topes
She lowered her standards by raising her glass
Her courage, her eyes and his hopes . . .

How did madeira come to be linked with the wiles of elderly rakes, so that no man now could offer a girl a glass of it without hearing an admonitory voice whispering in his ear and feeling himself twirling an imaginary mustache?

Madeira is such an innocent drink, and for a very long time one that arrived at adulthood only after severe trials. Originally unfortified, it was found to suffer on the long sea journey from its home in the mid-Atlantic; in the second part of the seventeenth century, it became clear that madeira fortified with brandy was somehow improved during the voyage to India, in the ships of the East India Company, and became even better if it made the round trip back again, gaining the status of *vinho da roda*.

As North America expanded, a new market for madeira grew, to such a degree that by 1800 fully a quarter of all madeira was being sold there; the Declaration of Independence was sealed with a toast of madeira in 1776.

But history and biology dealt madeira some harsh blows. First powdery mildew and then the phylloxera louse almost obliterated the vineyards; production had hardly got back to normal when first the Russian Revolution struck in 1917 and then the Volstead Act of 1919 brought Prohibition to America. Madeira never recovered its position in the market, and now there are a mere handful of shippers.

The most-planted varietals used in madeira are the Tinta Negra Mole and the Complexa grapes, though the traditional Sercial, Bual, Malvasia (Malmsey), and Verdelho grapes, which produce far better-quality Madeira, are making something of a comeback. Modern methods of production—particularly versions of the *estufa* system, which mimic the effect of the round-trip sea voyages that fell out of use in the early twentieth century—produce cheaper and medium-quality wines, while the best are still allowed to mature naturally in "lodges" for twenty years or more.

As the authors of the *Oxford Companion to Wine* point out, "Madeira is probably the most robust wine in the world." There's practically nothing that can go wrong with it. Indeed, the opposite may even be true: the infamous monk, rake, and orgiast Rasputin, having eaten a plate of cakes, each containing enough cyanide to kill a normal man, was given a glass of even more heavily poisoned madeira; he sipped it like a connoisseur and demanded more, on account of a "slight irritation" in his throat; the second glass seemed to soothe him and he asked his poisoner, Prince Yusupoff, to sing to him. (It took another song, five shots through the heart with a revolver, and his head battered in with a lead-loaded cane before Rasputin finally expired. *Do not try this at home.*)

Whatever their powers in that case, it is certainly true that the best madeiras are almost immortal themselves and can age in the bottle almost indefinitely. And as a bonus, a bottle of good madeira can last for several months after opening, although we personally have never put it to the test; it seems rather pointless to just leave it there, as the reader will surely agree.

But therein lies our seducer's fatal error. "Eager to carve one more notch / On the butt of his gold-headed cane," the cad declares that "once it is open you know it won't keep."

"It won't keep"? Feh. Exposed as a liar—to us, if not to the object of his evil lusts—the roué is defeated. The innocent rushes away down the corridor, his words—"Have some madeira, m'dear"—echoing in her mind:

> *Until the next morning, she woke up in bed*
> *With a smile on her lips and an ache in her head*

And a beard in her ear 'ole that tickled and said
"Have some madeira, m'dear."

Did religion save the California wine industry?

FROM ITS VERY beginnings in the seventeenth century, the United
States was a hard-drinking country. By the mid-nineteenth century, whether in the towns or out on the prairie, the drunkard
stumbling out of the saloon and reeling down the street was a familiar sight. Sentimental poems about children asking their fathers to stop drinking and songs about drink, degradation, and
death were widely popular, and slogans on the line of "Drink is
the curse of the working man" became a driving theme of soci-
eties that were set up to combat the demon rum. Chapters of
the Women's Christian Temperance Union (founded in 1874)
and then the Anti-Saloon League (founded in 1895) sprang up
around the country, encouraging individuals to "take the pledge"
against drink and lobbying the state legislatures to pass laws turning a state from wet to dry. The various Protestant churches were
strong allies of the movement. The goal evolved from temperance
to abolition, and immediately after the First World War, this was
accomplished: the Eighteenth Amendment to the U.S. Constitution, known as the National Prohibition or Volstead Act, became
law. Therefore, from January 16, 1920, until December 5, 1933,
the commercial production and sale of "intoxicating liquors" was
forbidden—and because the definition of an intoxicating liquor
was one with an alcohol content of 0.5 percent or higher, wine
was caught in the net.

It was the California wine industry, by far the largest in the
country, that got hit in the stomach. There were about seven
hundred wineries in the state and most of them soon closed
down, with the winemakers receiving no compensation. Many
of the wineries were simply broken up. The situation was not
the same for growers, however, because not only did vineyards

continue to be tilled, but the acreage doubled between 1919 and 1926. This curious anomaly can be explained by three loopholes in the law: the "fresh grape deal," sacramental wine, and medicinal wine. The first arose out of Section 29, which allowed the householder to make "nonintoxicating cider and fruit juices exclusively for use in his home" up to a limit of 200 gallons; because there was no explicit ban, it was interpreted as allowing home winemaking. Thousands of railway carloads of grapes headed east each year at vintage time to meet the demand, which came in particular from immigrant families living all over the country. Leon D. Adams in *The Wines of America* gives an account of American ingenuity in evading unpopular laws: packages of pressed grapes, called wine bricks, were shipped to these domestic winemakers, along with a yeast pill that the purchaser was advised not to use, "because if you do this, this will turn into wine, which would be illegal." The premium was on red grapes that could be shipped safely, with the result that plantings of Cabernet Sauvignon and Pinot Noir were pulled up and replaced with sturdier, if decidedly inferior, grape varieties such as Alicante Bouschet, Carignan, and Petite Sirah. Vineyards of first-class white wine grapes virtually disappeared during the 1920s. In other words, bad grapes drove out good, as far as winemaking was concerned.

The second loophole was the making of sacramental wine for both Christian and Jewish congregations for use in religious ceremonies. A number of Irish and Italian wineries had close relations with members of the Roman Catholic hierarchy, and they continued to make wine all through the period. But however many Christian priests and pastors of various sorts there were who required wine for holy communion, their numbers could not match those of rabbis. Again according to Adams, there was a remarkable revival of religious fervor during the 1920s: "The Jewish faith requires the religious use of wine in the home. Anybody could call himself a rabbi and get a permit to buy wine legally, merely by presenting a list of his congregation. Millions of all faiths and no faith became members of fake synagogues, some without their knowledge when the lists were copied from telephone directories."

The third loophole was medical. It was legal both to make and to sell wine for medicinal purposes, and there was an astonishing increase in illnesses that required treatment with, for example, Paul Masson's "Medicinal Champagne." Of course, brandy had been used for medicinal purposes for centuries, so the concept was not wholly alien.

The period of Prohibition saw a sharp increase in criminality, with the term *bootlegger,* used to refer to someone who smuggles liquor and other alcoholic drinks, coming into wide use. Respect for the law appeared to be collapsing, and increasing numbers of Americans became fearful about the threat to the very nature and fabric of the United States. In the 1932 presidential election, a plank in the Democratic Party's platform called for the repeal of Prohibition, and with Democratic victory, the forces for repeal triumphed. The Twenty-first Amendment to the Constitution repealed the Eighteenth, and from December 6, 1933, Prohibition was no more.

Most of the wineries in California, however, appear to have been caught off guard, and only a very few had stocks of decent wine on hand to sell to a thirsty public. Those that were rapidly reopened were very poorly equipped, with broken and rusty machinery and premises contaminated with disease. The wine made in these situations was, naturally, dire. This did not help sales. Indeed, of the 800 wineries that were reopened or newly established by 1934, only 212 were still in business four years later. Another difficulty with which wineries had to cope was a profound change in the style of wine that the majority wanted to drink. Before Prohibition, the preference had been for dry wine; thirteen years later, the situation was reversed, and by 1934, sweet wine, often fortified, outsold dry wine by three to one. This situation worsened considerably over the next several decades, so California was producing, and Americans were drinking, (often bad) sweet wine rather than dry.

In short, Prohibition came very close to destroying the California wine industry. It drove away a half generation of young winemakers, who had to make a living in other ways. It took a generation or more to grub up the inferior vines and replace them with new plantings of classic wine grapes. It destroyed a growing American taste for good wine, replacing it with a taste for bad, often sweet, wine: most Americans who drank wine at all during Prohibition drank only homemade wine of, at best, indifferent quality. The requirements of religious observation did indeed help to save enough of the industry to enable it to live and fight another day, but considering that organized religion had been a strong force behind the success of Prohibition in the first place, it seems only fair. The fact that religious observance appeared to require, or at least to accept, distinctly inferior sweet wine can only be regretted.

Why does Château Palmer have an English name?

THE SHORT ANSWER to this question is, because an Englishman named it after himself. Before this is condemned as unwarranted self-aggrandizement, however, it should be remembered that from the end of the seventeenth century, it became something of a habit to add one's own name to an estate that produced very good wine—the renaming of Branne-Mouton as Mouton-Rothschild in 1853 is but one example. Major-General Charles Palmer was born in the city of Bath Spa in 1777 and was educated at Eton and Christ Church, Oxford. When he was nineteen, his father purchased a commission for him in the 10th Hussars, the Prince of Wales's Own, which was a light cavalry regiment. He served throughout the Peninsular War from 1807 to 1814, and fought at the Battle of Waterloo in 1815. In February 1811, he became aide-de-camp to the Prince of Wales, the Prince Regent, the future King George IV. In 1813 he became lieutenant colonel of the 23rd Dragoons (heavy infantry), colonel in 1814, and major general in 1825. In 1814, after Napoleon's first surrender, Palmer arrived in France with the British commander in the Peninsula, the future Duke of Wellington. Parliament had voted Palmer £100,000 "as the representative of his father," John Palmer, who had invented the system of mail coaches, thereby providing a safer and more regular method of delivering the post. Palmer was to use this to buy property in France.

Palmer was known in London as a ladies' man. In France, he was dazzled by a beautiful young widow, Mme. Marie de Gascq, who wished to sell her late husband's estate in the Médoc, Château de Gascq. This was primarily a fine vineyard—it had no château as such. The story goes that during a three-day coach ride with her from Lyon to Paris—which has been referred to as "turbulent"—she convinced Palmer to purchase it. He did so, for the attractive price of 100,000 francs, and immediately renamed it Château Palmer. (David Peppercorn takes a more austere view, suggesting that Palmer's attention was directed to the property by one of the *courtiers*—brokers—of Bordeaux.) He threw himself into developing and extending his property, buying over the following seventeen years land and buildings in the communes of Cantenac, Issan, and Margaux. Indeed, by the time he sold it, it had grown from a small property to become one of the larger estates of the Médoc.

According to Captain H. R. Gronow in his *Reminiscences and Reflections*, published in parts from 1862 to 1866, Palmer supplied samples of his wine at a dinner for the Prince Regent to taste, in the hope that he would make it fashionable. Unfortunately, this did not work: the Prince preferred his usual version of claret fortified with some Hermitage, and he advised Palmer to experiment and make some better wines. According to Gronow,

> General Palmer, feeling it his duty to follow the advice of the Prince, rooted out his old vines, planted new ones, and tried all sorts of experiments, at an immense cost, but with little or no result. He and his agent, in consequence, got themselves into all sorts of difficulties, mortgaged the property, borrowed largely, and were at last obliged to have recourse to usurers, to life assurances, and every sort of expedient, to raise money . . . the accumulation of debt to the usurers became so heavy, that he was compelled to pass through the Insolvent Court.

There is an alternative version, partly based on Palmer's obituary in the *Gentleman's Magazine* of 1851. After the war, Palmer lived primarily in England: in 1808, at the death of his father, he succeeded him as the mayor of Bath and as the local MP, a position he held, even during the war, from 1808 to 1826 and again from 1831 to 1837. He also inherited the proprietorship of the Theatre Royal, Bath. His estate in France, which he spared no expense to develop and improve, was managed by his *régisseur*, Jean Lagunegrand, whose salary was as high as that of any of his profession in the Médoc. Palmer concentrated on promoting his wine in England, taking advantage of his connections at court and his charm. Because of its increasingly high quality, "Palmer's claret," according to Gronow, was much sought after by London clubs, and was particularly appreciated by the Prince Regent. This makes sense, given that Palmer had been aide-de-camp to the Prince and later his crony even before the prince became King George IV, and joined him in his love of fine food and wine. (This relationship, however, does not preclude the prince's having possibly told him that a bit more stomach in the wine would make it even better.) Even after the death of the King, Palmer spared no expense in providing himself and his friends with gastronomic feasts. This increasingly ruinous way of life was partly responsible for his reluctant decision to sell Château Palmer.

There was more to it than his desire for good dinners, of course. He had devoted much of his capital to developing Palmer, and it was now producing a great wine. But the high cost of running the estate was aggravated by economic difficulties in France as well as by the high duties, which damaged trade. His financial position declined alarmingly, and his wife left him; he lost his seat in Parliament. Things were brought to a head by a run of bad vintages, and in 1843 he sold Château Palmer. His death in 1851 prevented his seeing its inclusion in the 1855 Bordeaux classification (see p. 62). Unfortunately, the fact of Château Palmer being in receivership in 1855 and thus in the throes of reorganization was, according to Edmund Penning-Rowsell, probably responsible for its relegation to the second half of the *troisième grand cru* classification (the reorganization of Mouton-Rothschild in 1855 may also have been responsible for its listing as only a *deuxième cru*). It is arguable that its quality should have accorded it a position at the top of the *deuxième crus*, a position that many critics and wine lovers believe it deserves today. Its highly regarded quality was underlined by the fact that the new owners did not change the name.

Can the war on *terroir* be won?

ONLY IN THE MINDS of romantics and New Age pastoralists is Nature benign and in any way on our side. It may be a truism to remind ourselves that we are a part of nature, and that nature doesn't give a fig for us; equally, it is at best euphemistic and at worst delusional to talk of "saving the earth." The earth will shrug us off if we become too troublesome, and do perfectly well without us: what we mean, really, is saving our own sorry skins.

Nobody knows this better than farmers, and few farmers know

this better than the wine growers of Australia, where a combination of circumstances has threatened to halt, and even throw rapidly into reverse, the extraordinary way in which Australian wines have conquered the world over the last couple of decades.

It seems extraordinary that an underground ocean, its origins lost in the darkness of geological deep time, could affect the price of wine today on the other side of the world; but that world is increasingly and inextricably interconnected, however, and sometimes the past comes back to bite us.

The fertile southern tablelands of Australia—including the great wine-growing regions along the Murray and Darling rivers—lie upon just such a subterranean sea. Once they thought it came to the surface, and expeditions were launched to find the so-called Great Inland Sea, at the cost of many lives. The quest was in vain. The Great Inland Sea doesn't exist. But its legacy does. Beneath the soil lie deep deposits of heavily salt water. For millions of years, it simply didn't matter: native species evolved to cope with the salinity of the soil, and plants and geology lived in balance.

But then came the Europeans, and with the Europeans came European crops—particularly the grain and the grape. These, unable to handle the salt levels, needed irrigation, and the rivers were there to provide it. But the cost was high. The water for irrigation sank lower than the natural freshwater from the rains; as one farmer put it, we were pouring three feet of fresh water on land designed to cope with ten inches. And so the freshwater leached down, dissolving the lower levels of highly salty earth and seeping into the saltwater tables. Fresh and salt began to mix, and the saltwater rose to the surface or into the waterways. The results were potentially catastrophic: as one water engineer told us over ten years ago, "By the time you've realized the problem, you've missed the boat for the solution."

And just to make absolutely sure that we realize the indifference of nature, the "Big Dry" of 2007 posed an equal threat to the region's wine growers, promising to halve the 2008 grape harvest from 2 million metric tons to between 800,000 and 1.3 million. Australians seldom refer to "drought," preferring to talk about "a bit of a dry spell," but at the time of writing, the *D*-word was being bandied about freely.

Yet there is something about viticulture that brings out the best of human ingenuity. Partly it's the sheer figures involved today. Australia earned $1.9 billion from wine exports in 2006, exporting 176 million gallons, 40 percent to Britain and 30 percent to the United States. The majority was exported by Australia's largest wine company, Southcorp, which owns well-known labels such as Penfolds, Lindemans and Rosemont Estate, and nearly 2.5 million acres of vineyards (and whose biggest single customer is the U.K. supermarket chain Tesco); but individual winemakers, as well as selling to the big shippers, are producing small but increasingly high-quality house wines of their own.

This is currently all under threat: some growers are allowed to take only 10 percent of the water they would normally use for irrigation. As crop yields fall, prices increase; the good-quality, mass-produced "clean-skin" wines that Australia has become famous for will no longer be such excellent value. There is no way out of the economic loop.

Yet the reversal of the salination process in the Murray/Darling Basin has been hailed as an example to the rest of Australian agriculture. Tammy Van Wisse, of the Murray Darling Rescue project, described salinity as "arguably the greatest environmental threat facing Australia today. No one is immune. Salinity is spreading like cancer." The farmers of the Murray River have seen that cancer halted by a combination of engineering works and the management of water flows, and a national campaign is now encouraging the planting of perennial crops, trees, and salt-tolerant species such as *Atriplex amnicola* and a hybrid gum tree whose name clearly explains its most prized quality: the Saltgrow.

Individual vines are drip-fed water—each one gets precisely what it needs and no more.

Whether it will be enough remains to be seen. But the two commonest phrases among Australia's farmers are "no worries" and "she'll be right." These originated from a time when even the simplest of things was a big worry and whether she'd be right or not was always questionable. The Australians know what they're talking about. But nature is a hard taskmistress, and the war on *terroir* goes on.

How did steam drive Toulouse-Lautrec to absinthe?

THINK OF A fin-de-siècle French café and the chances are you think not of wine but of absinthe, a strange spirit invented by the inappropriately named Dr. Pierre Ordinaire in 1792. He offered it as a panacea; containing the egregious-tasting anise and, more important, wormwood (which contains a psychoactive compound, thujone), absinthe was modestly successful.

But what happened in the next hundred years that caused absinthe first to triumph, then to be seen as a threat to health and French civilization? And why did the French government eventually ban it from sale in France, a ban that continues to this day?

First, it should be said that absinthe is perhaps not the most benevolent of drinks. Taken to anything resembling excess, thujone has a tendency to cause a strange disorientation and even hallucinations. Not for nothing was it nicknamed *La Fée Verte*— the Green Fairy.

Nor do artists' representations of its devotees inspire great joy. Manet's painting of 1867 shows a solitary absinthe drinker, with shaggy beard, tall, battered hat, and a strange smeared expression, beside his glass of absinthe: the drink has taken on the *louche*—the pearlescent milkiness that the spirit acquires when mixed with water. He himself, like the room he's in, is out of focus: brown, blurred and bleary. Nine years later, Degas's *Absinthe Drinkers* are faring no better: they sit side by side on a hard bench before cold marble tables, both looking ahead, disconnected from the world and from each other. Perhaps the most dispiriting is Picasso's 1901 painting: an angular and seemingly anguished woman in a blue dress, her thin arms and bony hands wrapped around herself. In front of her are the absinthe glass and a blue water fountain; otherwise she is as utterly alone as can be. The only glamorous absinthe painting we know of is by the Czech artist Viktor Oliva. It hangs in the Café Slavia in Prague and shows us a man in evening dress gazing at the human-sized figure of the curvaceous, alluring *fée verte*; in the background, another smartly dressed man is approaching—a friend, perhaps, who will find little companionship in the drinker, who is already in a world of illusions.

Not, then, a companionable drink; not a promoter of commensality or conversation. The paintings of absinthe drinkers depict it more as a drug than as a drink, more like opium than like wine.

To find out the reason for the absinthe craze, we need to wind the clock back to the North American colonies of the seventeenth century. The French colonists in Florida first experimented with *Vitis vinifera*, the European wine grape. It was not a success, and they did not quite know why. But in due course they had more luck with native grapes.

They continued experimenting with hybrids, but the idea that *vinifera* was no good in America persisted, despite its doing well in California.

Unknown to them, the French Americans had made a mistake. The problems with *vinifera* were being caused by an aphid, the North American grape phylloxera. This, they failed to notice, was for a number of reasons. One is that phylloxera kills European grapes by injecting a poison into the vine, which swells and eventually kills the small roots. It behaves differently on North American vines, living mainly on the leaves, where it causes harmful galls but affects the roots much less badly. Another aspect of its behavior is that, feeding on the roots of *vinifera*, the phylloxera aphid will rapidly abandon ship when the osmotic pressure in the now-diseased root falls. Dig up the dead vine and there's nothing to see: the aphids have long gone.

Viticulture is an international business, and almost from the outset, European growers were experimenting with American vines. Yet there was no hint of phylloxera until the early 1860s, when Pujault, in the Languedoc, fell victim to a *malade inconnu*, an "unidentifiable sickness." This spread from vine to vine, and by the third year most were inexplicably dead, their roots decayed and blackened.

In 1868 the pharmacist J. E. Planchon, a hero of the French wine industry, discovered the link between the small yellow aphid and the dying vines. But as so often, opinions varied, and many believed the aphids were an effect of the disease, not the cause. It wasn't until 1870 that the American Charles V. Riley demonstrated that the phylloxera aphid was responsible for the leaf blight on American vines *and* the root disease in Europe. Furthermore, the odd life cycle of the aphid made the usual methods of attack ineffective. Laliman and Bazille came up with the idea that eventually worked: grafting *vinifera* onto resistant American rootstocks. It was not a new idea—the Spanish had been doing something similar in Mexico since the early sixteenth century—but it worked, and the Herculean task of reconstitution began throughout France.

The effects of phylloxera were dreadful for small French wine growers, many of whom emigrated—to the eventual benefit of the world's wines. At the time of the outbreak, too, wine growers were responding to skyrocketing demand by overplanting, growing inferior grapes, and growing them in unsuitable terrain. Much of the quality of today's wines, and many of the varietals we now take for granted, might simply not have existed had it not been for the phylloxera aphid. To call it a blessing in disguise is over-egging the pudding, unquestionably; still . . .

But back to the cafés of Paris. The first thing to happen when phylloxera began its devastation in France was that wine became scarcer and the price went up. The *vie bohème* of Paris, on the other hand, was not about to stop. It simply needed another fuel, and absinthe won the day. Centered upon the Moulin Rouge in Montmartre, at the heart of the Parisian red light zone, so marvelously chronicled by the stunted, aristocratic, ungainly, and hopelessly alcoholic Toulouse-Lautrec, the absinthe craze spread unstoppably. Even if not drunk in the form of Toulouse-Lautrec's *terre-tremblant*—"earth shaker," made of half absinthe and half cognac—but consumed in the usual way, with five parts of water slowly dripped through a sugar lump held in a pierced spoon to provoke the *louche* and sweeten the bitter taste of wormwood, absinthe was an unforgiving drink. In 1910, the French drank 9.5 million gallons of the stuff, and the Swiss banned it. In 1912, the Americans banned it, and in 1915 the French government decided that, far from being a specific against malaria for the troops, it was responsible for mass desertions from the trenches; that, together with pressure from the French wine lobby, anxious to regain its status as provider of the national drink, meant that the French banned it, too.

The draftsmen of the French law had, however, made one tiny mistake: they had banned the sale of absinthe in France but not the manufacture. After a ruling from the U.K. government allowing British companies to sell absinthe in any European country where it was not specifically banned, *La Fée* absinthe went into production in Paris.

We asked how steam had indirectly driven Toulouse-Lautrec to absinthe. Recall that the French colonists had been experimenting in Florida since the mid-seventeenth century; recall, too, that vines had been across the Atlantic for wine-growing experiments for much of the time since then. Why was it only in the 1860s that phylloxera first began its devastation of the French vineyards?

The answer is almost certainly that it was only after 1838 that regular steamship crossings of the Atlantic were established. In the days of sail and the early days of steam (the first steamship to make the crossing, the *Savannah*, in 1819, only had a tiny 90 hp auxiliary engine), the voyage took just under a month: too long for the aphids to survive. By 1838, the *Great Western* took half that time, and the subsequent generation of iron-hulled, screw-driven steamships competed furiously for the Blue Riband for the fastest passage.

Finally, because of the speed of the new steamships, the aphids could survive the transatlantic voyage. The stage was set for disaster, and disaster came onstage and made its bow.

When is rot "noble"?

THERE IS A fungus with a Jekyll-and-Hyde personality that grows on grapes: *Botrytis cinerea*. Given the right autumn weather conditions—cool misty mornings and warm sunny afternoons—the result can well be botrytis bunch rot. If the grapes are unripe or damaged, the result is the disastrous gray rot, which can destroy both quality and quantity. If, however, the grapes are white, ripe, light-skinned, and healthy, the result is likely to be "noble rot" (*pourriture noble* in France, *Edelfäule* in Germany). Grapes affected by noble rot look disgusting—shriveled, dotted with light brown spots, and covered with a gray dust that looks like ash (hence *cinerea*). Thin-skinned grapes such as Furmint, Riesling, Sémillon, and Chenin Blanc are particularly susceptible to noble rot, and each of them also has the necessary acidity to balance the intense sweetness of the botrytized juice. They can produce glorious wines, among which are Hungarian Tokaji Aszú, German Beerenauslese and Trockenbeerenauslese, and French Sauternes and Quarts de Chaume (from the Loire). The grapes develop this condition individually, so grapes on the same bunch shrivel unevenly. This means that pickers have to walk through the vineyard time and time again (*tries*), picking the grapes one by one. Unavoidably, wines made from these grapes are expensive.

Grapes affected by noble rot produce some of the greatest and longest-living wines in the world. The oldest is Tokaji Aszú, which comes from northeast Hungary. The story goes that in 1650, the priest on the estate where the old castle of Tokaji stands, who was also the winemaker, delayed the harvest because of the fear that the Turks were about to attack. While the bunches hung on the vines, some were attacked by the fungus. They were then pressed and fermented separately from the other grapes, and the result was a wine of unexpected flavor and character, which rapidly became the wine of kings and a diplomatic weapon in the hands of the Austrian emperor, who took over the estates as his own.

In Germany, the first making of a wine from botrytized grapes is traditionally attributed to Schloss Johannisberg in the Rheingau in 1775. It was owned by the abbot of Fulda, and the grapes could not be picked without his permission. The winemaker looked at the grapes and sent a courier to Fulda to tell the abbot that on the day the courier returned to the *Schloss,* the grapes would be ready to be picked. The journey there and back normally took fourteen days, but for reasons that nobody knows, the journey this time took much longer. By the time the courier did return, the grapes of Schloss Johannisberg were rotten. Nevertheless, wine was made, and, stunned by its sweetness, acidity, and floral spiciness, the abbot and the winemaker agreed that this wine, which was probably a Beerenauslese, should be made whenever it was possible.

In France, there is less conviction as to when botrytized wines were first produced. The utterly delicious wine Quarts de Chaume in the Loire, possibly the longest-lasting wine in the world, has arguably been made since the medieval period; those of Sauternes have been produced since the eighteenth century. It is a curious fate for the other wines that Sauternes is the most widely known, since they are at least as delicious. Does this reflect the power of public relations?

How would rhinos do conjuring?

YES, IT IS a strange question . . . but no, we have not taken leave of our senses. In fact, it's our senses that lead us to ask the question, and in particular, the most important sense in judging wine, which also happens to be our weakest: the sense of smell.

We'll keep the rhino in the back of our mind for a moment. Let's think about ourselves first. We are, primarily, creatures of sight. Hearing comes second; then taste, touch, and, finally, poor underprivileged smell.

Yet smell is more important than we think. When we taste wine—or, indeed, anything else—all we can really taste are five basic categories: sweet, sour, salt, bitter, and *umami*, the last a Japanese word for what the Western palate might describe as "meaty" or "savory" and found, for example, in miso, Roquefort, ketchup, mushrooms, and broccoli.

Those five are the only things we have taste buds for. Everything else we think we're tasting, we're actually smelling.

And in comparison with most mammals, we're pretty appalling at it.

Not our fault: our olfactory lobe is a shriveled little thing, withered away by thousands of years of evolution. But to improve upon our pathetic nasal patrimony, we need training. A Master of Wine's nose is cultivated, by years of practice and experience, to make fine differentiations that mystify the beginner, who may suspect either trickery or a sort of exquisite boasting. The vocabulary of wine writers has become an object of satire, with its knowing murmurings of pencil shavings and raspberries, of leather and petrol, apples, hay, blackcurrants, and indeed (some say) the drift of aircraft hydraulic fluid from the top of a good gewürztraminer.

But what other choice is there?

One of the problems we face is that, being visual animals, so many of our words are based on visual experience. We all know when something's green or rusty or sun-bleached, when it creeps along or rushes past in a blur, whether it's tall or round or angular.

But we can only summon up words to describe smells by comparing them to something of which we already know the smell. The problem isn't just for wine writers: restaurant reviewers, for example, struggle terribly to describe the taste (mostly, of course, the smells) of what they are eating, and resort to talking about how it was cooked, how it looked, what was in it, and what the dining room was like. The late John Diamond, journalist and husband of the celebrity cook Nigella Lawson, had almost no repertoire of descriptive language for food; his wife observed calmly over lunch one day that it was "a little dispiriting to be married to a man whose only responses to what you fed him were 'Yum' or 'Ugh.'"

The other profession that needs an accurate vocabulary of olfaction is, of course, the "noses" or perfumers whose art or craft surrounds us all the time, mostly unnoticed unless we encounter something particularly strident. (A perfume called Giorgio Beverly Hills was popular in the 1980s. It had all the subtlety of a military brass band exploding in a thunderstorm, and induced one of New York's grander restaurants to have a subtle but unmissable sign on its door reading "No Pipes, No Cigars, No Giorgio.")

Interestingly, perfumers go about it in a different way from oenophiles. Instead of dismantling the olfactory picture in terms of what it reminds your readers or listeners of, you build it up from individual ingredients you identify by what they remind *you* of.

The budding perfumer, for example, will be handed a tiny phial of *concrète de jasmin* and asked to do two things: first of all, to write down in a notebook the *first thing she thinks of* when she smells it; and, second, to describe it in relation to other smells and sensations. The scientist-turned-perfumer Luca Turin, the subject of Chandler Burr's *The Emperor of Scent*, quotes the fragrance scientist Gunther Ohloff on the rare and precious ambergris. Ohloff, who, he says, "probably knew more about ambergris than anyone before or since," calls it "humid, earthy, fecal, marine, algoid, tobacco-like, sandalwood-like, sweet, animal, musky and radiant."

But the actual entry under *ambergris* in Ohloff's notebook is something we don't know. It's private. His notebook is the most valuable—and the most personal—document a perfumer has. Entries *there* are very different. Here are some real ones: "the inside of an expensive lady's handbag"; "the sandstone dugout when I was little"; "wet hay"; "the crowd climbing up to Great Zimbabwe"; "the crush bar at the Royal Opera House"; "sunlight on old tarred ships' ropes"; "toffee apples at the Goose Fair"; and "teenagers' deodorant."

Who would have thought that they refer, respectively, to orris root, vetiver, coumarin, castoreum, dihydromyrcenol, *immortelle sauvage*, Maltol, and the dreadful Calone?

Ambrette, nitro musks, rose absolute, geranium, civet, menthyl lactate, sandalol, linalool, oakmoss, geraniol . . . the list runs into thousands of raw molecules, with more being captured by gas chromatography and "headspace technology" (you put a lid over, say, a flower and titrate its essence) and synthesized in massive multinational fragrance houses such as Firmenich, IFF, and Givaudan. And the would-be "nose" has to know them all and be able to retrieve them from his or her olfactory memory.

So the world of perfumery is a topsy-turvy version of the wine connoisseur's olfactory landscape. A perfumer will sniff a fragrance and think, "Rotten grapefruit, grandma's kitchen, the garden at La Masure, macaroons, oak bark, wet grass, tomcats," and, from this, compile the list of ingredients that went into it. The wine lover has no such luxury. She *knows* what went into it: grapes. And so the language must work backward, from the glass to the outside world.

The good news, of course, is that it can be taught. Once you have had your attention drawn to the odor of crushed violets at the base of Chanel No. 5, you will always notice it there in future. Once you know that petrol scent of a good Riesling, you will be able to identify it on the spot. Sometimes, of course, it doesn't help; the hydraulic fluid of a gewürztraminer is something you'll just have to take our word for.

And what does a rhinoceros have to do with the subject? Simply this: a rhinoceros lives in an olfactory world. Eyesight is way down on his list of useful senses. Even time is different for the rhino, who inhabits a sort of spectral world, a world in which the instantaneous demarcation between what's here now and what was here a moment ago simply does not exist. Where we see an empty room, a rhino would smell it crowded with ghosts, olfactory shadows of varying degrees of translucency. His impressions of the world alter not with the speed of light but with the speed of evaporation. Conjuring would mean nothing to a rhino: we see the dove disappear, but the rhino could smell it clearly, hidden in the false bottom of the magician's table.

So we might take a leap and presume that if rhinos had speech, their vocabulary would be heavily laden with words defining the tiniest distinctions between different smells and the way they blend and linger.

It's impossible to imagine what such a language would be like, of course, but that is in a way what wine writers are trying to achieve. No wonder they sometimes struggle.

To cork or not to cork: that is the question

A CORKED WINE is produced by the action of fungi on cork in the presence of chlorine, and is recognizable by the powerful mushroom, musty, or moldy aroma. Among the general wine-drinking public, there is no agreement on just how many corked bottles of wine there are, although everyone agrees that there must be lots of them. At the 2002 International Wine Challenge, for example, of the 12,000 bottles from around the world that were entered, 4 percent were corked—480 bottles. Even worse, at a 2008 tasting of the 2004 Chassagne-Montrachet Premier Cru (Blanc) organized by the magazine *The World of Fine Wine*, at which almost all of the top producers were represented, nearly 25 percent of the wines were either corked or oxidized. If one in four cans of baked beans was found to be faulty, there would be a huge outcry.

The question is, what should be done about it? There are currently three main ways to close a wine bottle: natural cork, plastic stoppers, or screw caps. Natural cork—the bark of *Quercus suber*, the cork oak—gradually replaced wooden stoppers, beeswax, or oil-soaked rags beginning in the early seventeenth century (although cork stoppers had been known to the Romans, the knowledge was lost during the medieval period). For its defenders, only natural cork ensures the proper aging of a good wine. They argue that minute quantities of air seep around and through the cork, allowing the wine to mature gradually, but that the tight fit of plastic corks prevents this. Who knows? There are as yet no publicized results of long-term comparative research to support their argument. Nevertheless, there is widespread agreement that for wines with the potential for long aging, such as the great clarets, Rhône wines, Italian Barolos, or German and Alsace rieslings, natural cork should be used.

However, in the early 1990s, supermarkets became tired of the high proportion of corked bottles and put pressure on producers to find an alternative. Over the following few years, more than ten different types of synthetic cork crowded onto the stage. There are substantial problems with plastic: there is some loss of flavor, technically known as "scalping"; there can be plastic taint; plastic-stoppered bottles lose sulfur dioxide too quickly, thereby encouraging oxidation and premature aging; and plastic corks are hard to extract from the bottle and impossible to push back in. As David Bird has written in *Understanding Wine Technology*, "There are those who would say that it is a pointless product—it is trying to imitate natural cork, which itself has imperfections." The main problem is aging. After eighteen months, the state of the wine in a plastic-corked bottle does begin to decline, but since relatively little supermarket wine is much older than that, this does not much matter. And for fast-moving, lower-value wine, such as that of large-scale New World producers or the supermarkets' own labels, plastic corks were for some years the closure of choice.

But times have changed, because now there is the screw cap, the most successful of the three in preventing oxidation. They give a perfect seal, do not cause taint or suffer from quality variation, and can be opened with the bare hand. Indeed, they have been known to protect white wine for ten years. The problem is presentation: do screw caps still imply a cheap wine or remind too many consumers of opening a bottle of vinegar?

The current state of play seems to be as follows. Most producers of premium wine, and especially of red wine, use natural cork, not least because they believe that their traditionally minded customers would be outraged if anything other than cork stoppered their bottles of wine. At a lower price level, and for wines which are meant to be drunk young, the use of plastic corks is still widespread, but they are increasingly being supplanted by screw caps. The screw cap was for some years primarily used for the cheapest wines, but today, here and there—especially in New Zealand, Australia, and California—increasing numbers of quality wine producers have adopted it. But the status hierarchy remains: do you prefer that the wine you drink be protected by a metal screw cap, a length of extruded plastic, or a piece of bark? The ceremony of removal of a cork by a skilled wine waiter is a wonderful one, even down to the suspicious sniffing of the cork, but the results seem to be depressingly uneven.

Does wine really provoke the desire and take away the performance?

IT'S BEEN the butt, as it were, of jokes since time immemorial, summed up by a drunken porter:

PORTER: Faith sir, we were carousing till the second cock: and drink, sir, is a great provoker of three things.

MACDUFF: What three things does drink especially provoke?

PORTER: Marry, sir, nose-painting, sleep, and urine. Lechery, sir, it provokes, and unprovokes; it provokes the desire, but it takes away the performance: therefore, much drink may be said to be an equivocator with lechery: it makes him, and it mars him; it sets him on, and it takes him off; it persuades him, and disheartens him; makes him stand to, and not stand to; in conclusion, equivocates him in a sleep, and, giving him the lie, leaves him.

Now we know it vulgarly as the "brewer's droop," but it might as well be the distiller's or, indeed, the vintner's, were it not for the popular understanding that there is something a little more delicate about the wine drinker's sensibilities that prevents him (for this particular affliction is confined to men) from making a human wineskin of himself to such an extent. It is, after all, "drink," as the Porter says; and there is no record of what they were carousing *on* "till the second cock." And "drink" in this case means alcohol: more accurately ethanol, or, as doctors waggishly call it, EtOH.

But is there any evidence that drink really *does* take away the performance? That it provokes the desire, taken in the right measure, seems unequivocal: "beer goggles," with their strange illuminating power of augmenting the beauty of whoever is seen through them, are available through the foot of a wineglass, too, and perhaps are even rosier (though again, the effect is attributed to beer as another tribute to the greater delicacy of the wine-bibber).

And the mechanism of these magic glasses is clear, too. Contrary to how it may initially seem, after that first soothing yet invigorating pair of glasses when the company grows more welcoming, the room warmer, and the wits sharper, alcohol is in effect a depressant. Even champagne, twinkling in its flute, hides a blackjack in its innocent *pétillance*, and in the heel of every fine burgundy lurks a thug with a sock full of wet sand.

We perceive it otherwise because the depressive effects of ethanol seem to work from high to low, in terms of brain function. First to go is that which makes us most human: our finely calibrated tool kit of social inhibitions. Then goes the judgment—just a little but certainly enough—then the volume control and, presently, spleech itselth; the legs wobble, balance fails, the gorge rises. And if all this is not enough (and by this point, as many of us may have experienced in youth, only a direct message from God would be enough) and the victim goes on drinking, eventually consciousness will recede and the sodden cerebellum may decide that breathing itself is no longer worth the effort.

We aren't concerned with such extremes here. We are not even venturing into the degree of drunkenness that makes so many of our city centers such hells of roaring and midriff after dark. Let us instead stop at the moment when the initial inhibitions have broken down. A man may spy a woman who, his judgment suspended by hock, suddenly appears to him the most beautiful creature he has ever seen. Normally, he would keep his counsel, but he drains another glass and weaves over to her; sober, he might say, "Hello," but, a little illuminated, he will say meaningfully, "Well, hel-*lo*," perhaps even with an invisible exclamation mark and question mark afterward, like this: "Well . . . hel-*lo*!?"

What will happen next is equally predictable. He will, unless rebuffed (which he will not be; she too is slightly lit up), bring them more wine; he will also gaze into her eyes. *Science has proven this.* People under a pleasant degree of intoxication make longer eye contact than the virtuously sober. Science has also proven that if two people of opposite sex (or two of the same sex, if that is their natural inclination) gaze into each other's eyes for more than about fifty seconds, a powerful and rationally inexplicable sense of attraction forms between them. (This is unlike what happens if you do the same experiment with two heterosexual men: after the same length of time, both report feeling a powerful, yet entirely unprovoked, desire to punch each other on the nose.)

And now the stage is set. Desire has been provoked. A couple more glasses, or, if at dinner, an armagnac for him and a green Chartreuse for her, and the curtain falls on the first act.

The second act takes place in a taxi; then in his, or her, apartment; then in his, or her, bedroom; and is none of our business.

The third act curtain rises upon a man with his head in his hands claiming that he must be tired—he has been working terribly hard recently—and a woman making soothing observations about how it's all right and not to worry, while the ghost of the Porter cackles knowingly in the background.

But *is there any truth in it?* Hunt through the libraries, trawl the Internet, and you will find thousands upon thousands of assertions that *so it is:* drink takes away the performance. Look more carefully, though, and it begins to acquire something of a slightly shady air. Dr. Irwin Goldstein, who founded the Institute for Sexual Medicine at Boston University Medical School, told a television audience that "alcohol use was actually not a statistical indicator of erectile dysfunction unless and until the alcohol consumption was fairly excessive. There are lots of reports that minor use of ethanol actually prevents vascular disease, which turns out to be probably the basic underlying dysfunction." In other words, a few drinks keep the pipes clear and should make things better, not worse. And the authoritative *Merck Manual of Geriatrics*—not, alas, a listing of the distinguished and venerable, but an extensive guide to the frailties of humanity under the scourge of time—does acknowledge that alcohol *may* be a contributory factor in *up to* 25 percent of cases, but it makes the same claim for anticonvulsants, anti-infective agents, antiarrhythmics, adrenergic blockers (centrally or peripherally acting), beta-blockers, calcium channel blockers, anxiolytics, antidepressants, antipsychotics, cocaine, lithium, narcotics, anticholinergics, acetazolamide, baclofen, cimetidine, clofibrate, danazol, disulfiram, interferon, leuprolide, naproxen, and others besides.

None of which, however, is known for provoking the desire; nor would they have made such a good speech for the Porter.

So the answer to our question is: it seems to, sometimes, but we don't really know why.

Yet what a fragile flower the act of love proves to be, particularly from the male's point of view. Cast by a harsh world in the character of ravening satyr, he is truly so delicate that the very elixir of a southern hillside needed to brace him up to approach his desire can prevent him from consummating it—though the reason would seem to be not alcohol itself but an *excess* of alcohol. Falling asleep, an attack of the whirling pits, a raging thirst, or an attack of nausea are equally effective at terminating a night of passion before it has begun. The fault (as Shakespeare almost observed) is not in our glass but in ourselves.

What was a "comet wine"?

DID YOU EVER briefly wonder what was meant (in "The Stockbroker's Clerk") when Dr. Watson says, "Sherlock Holmes cocked his eye at me, leaning back on the cushions with a pleased and yet critical face, like a connoisseur who had just taken his first sip of a comet vintage"? In the nineteenth century, French winemakers believed that comets were hot objects, and that this heat produced particularly good grapes. Therefore, they claimed, years when comets appeared were great vintage years. This conviction apparently began with the appearance of Flaugergues's Comet in 1811, which happened to coincide with a hot, dry summer. According to Michael Broadbent in his *Vintage Wine*, this "comet vintage" was possibly the greatest vintage of the nineteenth century throughout the European wine regions.

During the nineteenth century, the night skies appear to have been littered with comets, with at least three dozen of them making an appearance. The question was, did great vintages coincide with the appearance of comets? If one compares Broadbent's listing of outstanding wines of Bordeaux during this period, the answer is yes: 1811, 1825, 1844, 1846, 1847, 1848, 1858, 1864, 1865, 1870, 1875, and 1899. However, it is immediately noticeable that this is only a dozen years, and they do not include, for example, 1835, when Halley's Comet made its periodic appearance, nor the years of the Great Comets of 1843, 1861, and 1882.

However, with nearly every decade combining at least one great vintage with a comet, it is clear why the French wine brokers latched on to a great marketing opportunity, with advertisements in newspapers and entries in catalogues listing comet vintages: it was a claim that the wine-drinking public was apparently willing to believe.

What did Dr. Johnson challenge his Master to drink?

HERE BEFORE US as we write is a rare first edition of Dr. Johnson's epic 1755 *Dictionary* . . . no; let's give it the full ceremony of its title:

> A Dictionary of the English Language in which
> The WORDS are deduced from their ORIGINALS and
> ILLUSTRATED in their DIFFERENT SIGNIFICATIONS
> by EXAMPLES from the best WRITERS.

How does this most convivial and clubbable of men—he defined the word *club* as "an assembly of good fellows, meeting under certain conditions"—define *wine?*

Soberly enough.

"*WINE*," he writes: "The fermented juice of the grape," and that (compare the EU definition; see p. 7) is that. Straightaway, Johnson is off on a list of supporting quotations, beginning with Shakespeare ("The *wine* of life is drawn, and the mere lees / Is left this vault to brag of") and working through the Bible ("Be not amongst *wine*-bibbers, amongst riotous eaters"), Bacon ("Where the *wine*-press is hard-wrought, it yields a harsh *wine* that tastes of the grape-stone"), Sandys, Milton, Herbert, and Pope, ending with the satiric Swift ("If the hogshead falls short, the *wine*-cooper had not filled it in proper time").

His secondary entry is a quote from Arbuthnot, which goes straight to the point discovered by anyone who has ever had a glass of terrible homemade parsnip wine, and, indeed, by elephants, who allegedly throw fruit into water holes and come back later when it has fermented: "Preparations of vegetables by fermentations called by the general name of *wines*, have quite different qualities from the plant; for no fruit, taken crude, has the intoxicating quality of *wine*."

A modest enough explanation of one of the most far-reaching discoveries of all time, but then, surprisingly enough for the great conversationalist of his age, Dr. Johnson forswore his drinking, thereafter more likely than not to be confining himself to water when those about him were downing the stuff by the bottle. Yet there were few subjects on which he enjoyed conversing more than wine, one of which brought about his celebrated quarrel with the artist Sir Joshua Reynolds. In the middle of a discussion about wine at the house of General Paoli, Johnson, fueled on nothing more than water, suddenly bellowed, "I won't argue with you any more, Sir. You are too far gone." Far from taking it on the chin, the great painter snapped back, "I should have thought so indeed, Sir, had I made such a speech as you have now done." It wasn't the only occasion, either: at Richard Cumberland's house, Johnson asked for another cup of tea, only to be told by Reynolds that he had already had eleven cups. "Sir," roared the Great Bear, as he was known, "I did not count your glasses of wine. Why should you number up my cups of tea?" But the occasion ended in laughter.

Dr. Johnson, when not on his water diet, was known for the strength of his head and once famously drank thirty-six glasses of port at one sitting "with a sugar-lump in every glass" without showing any effects. But *port* could cover a multitude of wines, some of them sinful. When Johnson challenged his friend and benefactor, the wealthy brewer Henry Thrale, whom Johnson referred to as his "Master," to a drinking competition, it was not port he suggested. In the presence of Fanny Burney, he said:

I wish my Master would say to me, "Johnson, if you will oblige me, you will call for a bottle of Toulon," and then we will set to it, glass for glass, till it is done; and after that, I will say, "Thrale, if you will oblige me, you will call for another bottle of Toulon," and then we will set to it, glass for glass, till that is done; and by the time we should have drunk the two bottles, we should be so happy and such good friends, that we should fly into each other's arms, and both call together for the third!

Three bottles of Toulon might have been enough to set Thrale a-going—according to Johnson, "his conversation does not show the minute hand, but he strikes the hour very correctly"—but what actually was it that he was thinking of? Go into a restaurant or a bar now and call for a bottle of Toulon—we have conducted this experiment so that you do not have to—and you'll be met with blank looks. Explain that Toulon was, in the eighteenth century, a center of the French wine trade, and that the wines of Toulon would probably now, geographically, fall into the Côtes de Provence, and some light will dawn, resulting in the offer— the odds are still roughly four to one—of some light, dry rosé, the stuff of holiday memories on the Côte d'Azur. The Provençal wine growers are making efforts to move out of this frisky, slightly frou-frou ghetto, mindful perhaps of their heritage as arguably the most ancient wine-growing area of France; certainly the Provençal landscape of vines, olives, and lavender would have been familiar to the ancient Romans, though Narbonne disputes the claims of Marseilles to precedence in the matter. Whatever the historical truth, Provençal growers are leavening their Cinsaut- and Grenache-based rosés with some serious red wines. Two of the essential varietals in red and rosé Côtes de Provence, Mourvèdre and Tibouren, have ancient roots in the region, and Syrah has been identified as being the progeny of two other grapes from southeastern France, Dureza and Mondeuse Blanche. Somehow it is contrary to nature to imagine the Great Bear, the tremendous, squinny-eyed, skew-wigged, dropsical Johnson, planning to illuminate his and Mr. Thrale's friendship with the sort of cool rosé more suited to balmy evenings on restaurant terraces in Gordes or St. Paul de Vence, dreaming of selling up and moving to the sun. Far more satisfying to think of the two of them working happily through the third bottle of something more akin to a new-style Provençal red, ideally from Bandol, with Mourvèdre, Tibouren, and Syrah's forebears working in their veins.

And yet . . . Johnson was opinionated about wine, but no snob. After all, it was he who wrote to his friend Samuel Richardson asking to be rescued from the bailiffs. "I remember writing to him from a sponging-house"—where debtors were confined until their friends could spring them by paying their debts—"and was so sure of my deliverance through his kindness and liberality that, before his reply was brought, I knew I could afford to joke with the rascal who had me in custody, and did so, over a pint of adulterated wine, for which, at that instant, I had no money to pay." Conviviality and friendship, as ever, took precedence over what was in the bottle. Perhaps it was, after all, a skinny quotidian rosé he had in mind.

Why is hock linked to Queen Victoria?

ACCORDING to Dr. Johnson in his *Dictionary*, *hockamore* (the English rendering of *Hochheimer*) and its shortened form, *hock*, referred to "old dry strong Rhenish," that is, Rhine wines made primarily from the Riesling grape. This was in the eighteenth century, and England had been importing Rhenish wines since the medieval period—Samuel Pepys notes in his diary in the 1660s his regular visits to "Rhenish wine houses." In transport terms, it was an easy journey for the wine: by barge down the Rhine, stopping only to pay tolls at every passing castle, and by ship across the North Sea. Thomas Jefferson (see p. 34) noted in 1788 that the wines of Hochheim, along with those of Rüdesheim and Johannisberg, were the most expensive in the Rheingau, and indeed, hock was one of the world's most expensive wines in the eighteenth and nineteenth centuries. Michael Broadbent has pointed out that at the Christie's sale in 1808, a dozen bottles of "Very Old Hock" sold for over £10, the highest price for any wine at auction between 1766 and the 1880s.

Thus, before Victoria was even thought of, hock was a fashionable wine in England. Why, then, do wine catalogues ascribe to Victoria the responsibility for the wine's popularity? Most wine merchants do not claim to be historians, but the story of Victoria and her liking for hock is part of the wine trade's folklore. Undeniably her devotion to her consort, the German-born Prince Albert of Saxe-Coburg-Gotha, led her to embrace many things German, including their wines. When they traveled to Germany in 1850, they visited the town of Hochheim, and the linking of hock and Hochheim was obvious. And what royalty did, many others followed.

What is sad is the falling into desuetude of the term *hock* to refer to wines of quality. By the 1970s, a hock was a generic white German wine, usually sweetened, which could regularly be found in large bottles on the bottom shelves of supermarkets.

Ceremonial: shall we combine?

IF YOU SHOULD be invited to dine at High Table at one of Britain's oldest universities, your host may well ask this question, which is less sinister than you might think. "Combination" is one of the most appealing of the many wine-based ceremonies, and a sort of reversal of the old (and thankfully now defunct in civilized society) custom in which the women retire to the drawing room and the men stay behind at table to get blind drunk (in the eighteenth century) or to bore each other with talk of money and off-color jokes (the nineteenth and twentieth centuries).

College dining is, of course, collegiate in nature, with the students and Fellows (the senior members of the college) eating in the same room, generally simply called "Hall." But instead of the junior members being thrown out like so many ladies, the Fellows and their guests throw *themselves* out, retiring to drink wine—usually port, claret, or a sweet dessert wine.

In other words, they combine with each other. (Cynics say that the tradition arose so that the senior members could get blotto without setting a bad example to the juniors, though the more observant might say that it works both ways and is merely the civilized turning of a mutual blind eye. But things are more decorous these days, anyway.)

Customs vary. At Magdalene College, Cambridge, for example, people sit in groups of two or three at small occasional tables arranged in a semicircle, looking out over the courtyard and illuminated by candlelight, and the wines are brought round by the most junior Fellow present. The strict rule is that you may not, as you sip your claret and nibble your Bath Oliver biscuit, sit next to the people you were sitting with at dinner.

At other colleges, they proceed to another version of the dining table, where, as well as biscuits, there may be cheese, fruit, nuts, and a collegiate snuffbox; in these cases the wines are kept in circulation, and strictly in a clockwise direction, so that each person gets the bottle presented to his or her right hand (and hard luck if you're a southpaw).

Some years ago we had the good fortune to sit next to a distinguished woman, no longer young, who had acquired her husband—a lord, no less—by virtue of this tradition. He had invited her to High Table at his college, and after dinner, distracted by the presence of her beloved, she had inadvertently passed the wine—"a rather indifferent Sauternes," she said; "I remember it clearly"—the *wrong way*. The ancient don on her right was startled and perplexed, she said. Quite obviously he didn't know what to do at the sight of a bottle appearing by his left hand.

"Then I had a flash of inspiration," she said. "I noticed the old chap was in a wheelchair. So I stood up, took his brakes off—I was a nurse at the time, my dear, so I knew all about wheelchairs—and wheeled him an entire circuit of the table *in an anti-clockwise direction*. I thought that if he arrived at the wine anti-clockwise, it would be the same as if the wine had arrived at him clockwise. Saved the day. *Well.* My beau watched entranced and afterwards said it was the most impressive thing he'd ever seen, that it was quite clear that *I'd do,* and would I do him the honor of becoming his wife. So *that,* my dear, is how I became Lady ———."

Combining is seldom so literally interpreted. But it remains a charming tradition of commensality over wine. (And one small word of advice: there is no need for even the shyest to find themselves conversationally stuck. All you need to do is turn to your neighbor at such an occasion and say, "Tell me, what are you working on at the moment?" And he will tell you; boy, will he tell you.)

What wine is "pampered by the sun"?

GERMANY'S southernmost border runs in a wiggly line for 250 miles east-west at between 47°N and 48°N. This means that *all* of Germany's vineyards are north of the great French wine-growing regions of Burgundy, Bordeaux, and the Rhône. It is for this reason that Germany's production, like England's, is mainly of white wine. However, the southwest corner of the country, Baden, around Freiburg im Breisgau, is proud to be one of the hottest regions of Germany. To the visitor, Baden has almost a Mediterranean feel, despite its being a long way north of the sea. Here, three-quarters of the total acreage is given over to red grapes, primarily Pinot Noir, called Spätburgunder in Germany. The climate also means that Baden whites are generally more alcoholic than other German whites. This is because the sunshine enables the natural sugars in the grapes to rise to a higher level than is possible in the cooler north of Germany by harvest time, and the higher the sugar level, the higher the alcoholic strength.

Baden wine is promoted as *von der Sonne verwöhnt*, which translates as "pampered by the sun." As applied to children, the usual English translation of *verwöhnt* is "spoilt," but this translation would not, perhaps, convey exactly the nuance desired.

Was Pliny the first Robert Parker?

GAIUS PLINIUS SECUNDUS, known to posterity as Pliny the Elder, is probably remembered primarily for being killed, perhaps by sulfur fumes, perhaps by a heart attack, as a result of the eruption of Mount Vesuvius over Pompeii. But in his own day, for centuries thereafter, and among those today who are interested in the ingathering of knowledge, Pliny was famous above all for his *Naturalis Historia*. In its thirty-seven books, he surveys all of nature—animal, vegetable, and mineral, and sometimes human. He is indefatigable. His nephew and adopted son, Pliny the Younger, wrote about his uncle's work habits (*Letters* 3.5.14–16):

> In retirement only the time for the bath deflected him from his studies. (When I say "the bath," I mean when he was in the water, for when he was being scraped and toweled, he was

either listening to or dictating something.) When on a journey, as though freed from other preoccupations he devoted himself solely to study. His secretary sat by him with a book and writing-tablets; in winter his hands were shielded with gauntlets so that not even the harsh temperature should deprive him of any time for study. For this reason even when in Rome he was conveyed in a chair. I recall his rebuke to me for walking: "You could," he said, "have avoided wasting those hours." For he believed that any time not devoted to study was wasted. It was through such concentration that he completed those numerous volumes [of *Naturalis Historia*].

He clearly lived up to the conviction he wrote in the Preface to Book XVIII: *Vita vigilia est*—life is being awake.

Pliny was born in AD 23 and went through several careers. He was an equestrian or cavalry officer, serving in Germany; he then had a very active legal practice; following this, he was appointed to a number of high procuratorships—that is, he was a senior civil servant—in which he won a reputation for integrity. Finally, in semiretirement, he was given command of the Misenum fleet, that part of the Roman navy stationed in the Bay of Naples. His sense of duty plus his curiosity killed him: when Mount Vesuvius erupted on August 24, 79, he led a detachment to the disaster area, landed at Stabiae, went into the city, took a nap, left it too long, and, when he was dragged out to the beach, collapsed. It was this curiosity that drove him to learn, and duty that drove him to write up what he had learned. His literary work was carried out alongside his official work, which apparently did not suffer from a lack of his attention. His output was phenomenal, but all that remains is his *Naturalis Historia*.

Book XIV is devoted to the vine and wine. He lists, he describes, he considers, and he often pronounces. "But where," he asks, "can we better make a beginning than with the vine?" He describes the various ways of cultivating the vine, and follows this with a discussion, which is pages long, of the many varieties of grapes and their uses. He talks about famous wines of former times, the oldest of which was the wine of Maronea grown in the seaboard parts of Thrace, as described by Homer. He also celebrates a more recent vintage, the vintage of Opimius, called such because it was the year of the consulship of Lucius Opimius; this was 121 BC, and it was probably as memorable because it was also the year of the assassination of Gaius Gracchus "for stirring up the common people with seditions" or proposals for reforms. That year the weather was so fine and bright ("they call it the 'boiling' of the grape") that wines from that vintage, according to Pliny, still survived nearly two hundred years later. He did add, however, that they had "now been reduced to the consistency of honey with a rough flavor, for such in fact is the nature of wines in their old age." Nevertheless, if an amphora of this wine cost a hundred sesterces the year it was made, 160 years later a hundred sesterces would buy only one-twelfth of an amphora of the wine—"so large," he exclaims, "are the sums of money that are kept stored in our wine cellars! Indeed there is nothing else which experiences a greater increase of value up to the twentieth year—or a greater fall in value afterwards, supposing that there is not a rise of price." The Opimian vintage was an exception, because it continued to improve beyond twenty years—although clearly not for two hundred.

Pliny predated the 1855 classification technique by nearly two thousand years when he listed Italian wines in order of merit, for, he says, "who can doubt . . . that some kinds of wine are more agreeable than others, or who does not know that one of two wines from the same vat can be superior to the other, surpassing its relation either owing to its cask or from some accidental circumstance?" He then classifies Italian wines into first-, second-, third-, and fourth-class wines, other wines, and foreign wines. He does not, however, follow fashion blindly. Many commentators have exalted Falernian wine, and indeed, he remarks that "no other wine has a higher rank at the present day." Pliny, however, puts it into the second class, although he does praise the estate of Faustus because of "the care taken in its cultivation"; but, he adds, "the reputation of this district also is passing out of vogue through the fault of paying more attention to quantity than to quality." Modern parallels leap to mind.

Finally, he is firm on the vexed question of *terroir*. In his discussion of the areas in Italy where good wines were made, he gives Campania as an example of a region that, "whether by means of careful cultivation or by accident," good wines had recently been produced from new areas of cultivation. On the other hand, there were areas where decent wine would never be made, no matter what efforts were taken: "as for the wines of Pompei [*sic*], their topmost improvement is a matter of ten years, and they gain nothing from age; also, they are detected as unwholesome because of a headache which lasts till noon on the following day." Therefore, "these instances, if I am not mistaken, go to show that it is the country and the soil that matters, not the grape, and that it is superfluous to go on with a long enumeration of kinds, since the same vine has a different value in different places." In any case, "everyone has his own favorites," and "I would not deny that other wines also deserve a high reputation, but the ones that I have enumerated are those on which the general agreement of the ages will be found to have pronounced judgment."

So what can we say about Pliny as wine judge and wine writer? First of all, he was almost unbelievably hardworking; he also tended to castigate those whom he thought were not working as hard. His curiosity was capacious and his command of detail admirable. Although he was willing to admit that others might think differently, he clearly saw himself as having the last word. His work is still read with pleasure and profit two thousand years after his death: will the same be said of any of today's well-regarded wine writers two millennia hence?

Which Liebfraumilch isn't Liebfraumilch?

POOR LIEBFRAUMILCH has had a bad press in recent years, perhaps because of its associations with branded supermarket wines
such as Blue Nun, the sweetish, fruity, mass-market harbingers
of faux sophistication and nightmarish Abigail's Parties in carefully managerial housing estates.

Poor Liebfraumilch. You couldn't call it glamorous. Blue Nun's
main competitor in the 1970s, for example, was that icon of unso-
phistication, Mateus Rosé. And the fruity, low-acid Müller-
Thurgau varietal from which most cheap Liebfraumilch was made
was largely grown because it was a more profitable crop than
knobbly, proletarian old sugar beets. No, not glamorous.

Poor Liebfraumilch. Its name isn't even German, but a sort of
pidgin Deutsch; the real version would be Liebfrauenmilch—
"beloved lady's milk"—a reference to the Virgin Mary (just as the
Blue Nun herself bore striking resemblances to the traditional
iconography of Mary, but not enough to rouse the Catholics).

Despite its multiple, generic, and downscale by-blows, the
original Liebfraumilch, from the Liebfrauenstift-Kirchenstück,
the vineyards around the Liebfrauenkirche in Worms, can still
be had. But Madonna Liebfraumilch, as it is labeled, is not
a Liebfraumilch. It is far too posh for that, being officially a
"QmP"—a Qualitätswein mit Prädikat, the top level of the
German classification—while its déclassé relations are mere
Deutscher Landwein, one up from the bottom.

Poor Liebfraumilch.

What wines did Chaucer's pilgrims drink?

BORN THE SON and grandson of vintners (wine importers), Geof-
frey Chaucer, who lived from c. 1343 to 1400, was primarily a
civil servant, although of an exalted sort. He had married the
sister of the third wife of John of Gaunt, Duke of Lancaster and

younger son of King Edward III, and Gaunt's patronage was important in securing Chaucer's appointment to various positions. But Chaucer had another life, that of a reader, translator, and writer of books; *Canterbury Tales* is only his most widely known.

Wine was plentiful in England. Part of Chaucer's payment for some years was a jug of wine each day, while later on he was to receive a cask of wine each year. Wine makes a frequent appearance in the *Tales*, although what type of wine is often unclear. In the Prologue, for example, the Summoner drank strong red wine, while the Host at the Tabard, a high-class hostelry, provided strong wine for the group of pilgrims. What was it? The obvious answer should be red wine from Bordeaux, which at that time still belonged to the English Crown. But most Bordeaux wine was not "strong": rather, it was very light red (what the French called *clairet*) or even the color of a rosé. Indeed, Hugh Johnson in his *Story of Wine* points out that it was what the French called a *vin d'une nuit*. The grapes were trodden, and the wine fermented on the skins in the vat for no more than twenty-four hours—a single night—before the liquid was run off into barrels to ferment as a clear, pale juice. A small proportion of the must (juice) was left in the vat with the skins to become redder, but the resulting wine was too harsh and dark to serve on its own; some would be added to the paler wine to darken it and give it some "edge." Johnson compares it to modern Beaujolais Nouveau. The Tabard was too upmarket to give the pilgrims the inferior wine, and therefore it seems likely that Chaucer's "strong wine" must have come from elsewhere.

A strong possibility is that it was wine from Spain. From about 1250, wine was regularly shipped from Bilbao to Bristol, Southampton, and London. The best wines were very good: when prices were fixed by Edward III in 1364, the best Spanish wine cost the same as the best Bordeaux. Coming from a hot climate, the wines were high in alcohol and therefore strong. It is arguable, then, that the Host's strong wine was a good-quality, alcoholic red wine from Spain.

Chaucer mentions other wines, including the aromatic and flavored. One was Ypocras or Hippocras, drunk as an after-dinner digestif or served with cakes as a late-night collation. This was made with either red or white wine, although red was usually preferred, as its greater robustness was thought to aid digestion. According to *The Customs of London* (1811), you should take a quart of red wine, an ounce of cinnamon, a half ounce of ginger, a quarter of an ounce of white pepper, and half a pound of sugar, bruise the spices, and put the sugar, spices, and wine into a woolen cloth made for it. You then let it hang over a vessel until the wine has run through. Other recipes call for bringing the wine to a boil with the spices and honey (rather than sugar, which was relatively rare and expensive), straining it through a muslin bag, bottling it, and leaving it to mature for a month. The name came from Hippocrates's sleeve, which this bag was thought to resemble. Hippocras was clearly a type of mulled wine, and its popularity continued well into the seventeenth century, when Pepys enjoyed it. It evolved into hot punch, the eighteenth-century favorite in both Britain and the colonies.

Another heated and flavored wine that makes an appearance was clarree, which apparently took its name from *vinum claratum*, or clarified wine. The base here was sweet white wine, which was first boiled with honey, and to which were added cinnamon, cardamom, white pepper, and ginger; as with Hippocras, clarree was then strained and left to mature.

One wine mentioned by Chaucer, Vernage, was not a concoction as were the others. Rather, it was a wine of great luxury from Italy, and was made from the gentle pressing of dried bunches of grapes—in effect, from raisins. It was very sweet and relatively high in alcohol. By the early fifteenth century, however, it had practically ceased to be imported into England, although, according to one writer, it had a beautiful red color and aroma, it was not too sweet, and it had an exquisite taste. But it was too expensive to be widely available in public inns: only three out of some four hundred in London served it, and these were undoubtedly inns patronized by the Quality.

There are at least two possibilities for the indeterminate nature of the wines in *Canterbury Tales*. First of all, specific types of wine were usually irrelevant to the stories, and Chaucer himself reportedly did not care overmuch for wine. But the other was that having much detail as such was unusual, although the purchaser presumably did know the country of origin of the wine he bought. (But what *was* the Pardoner's "white wyn of Lepe," which was a "wyn of Spaigne"?) When you purchased wine, you usually depended on the merchant, ordering from him, say, five casks of wine from Gascony or a butt of malmsey or two casks of Rhenish. The merchant would then supply it, but it is doubtful whether a list of estates and appropriate tasting notes were included with the delivery.

What was the ambrosia of the gods?

THIS IS A question that's bound to come up sooner or later, often (in our experience) triggered by something special from Château d'Yquem or a particularly fine Tokaji, maybe a Banyuls or a glass of Klein Constantia. Whatever, the thing that sets them off— "Ah, the ambrosia of the gods!"—is usually something sweet and white.

Sometimes they may say *nectar* instead of *ambrosia*, but the truth is, it makes little difference: the words seem originally to have been used interchangeably, though *ambrosia* has some seniority in the matter. Subsequently, nectar seems to have become the drink of the gods, and ambrosia their food, but that's more from custom than precision—precision being unattainable because it's unlikely that there are any gods on Mount Olympus, and if there were, we wouldn't know what they drank.

The word *ambrosia*, in this context, may be one of those fascinating coincidences that give rise to false but enduring associations. It may be derived from the Greek for "immortal"—hence its association with the gods—but is far more likely to come from the same root as *amber* and to mean "sweet-smelling." A similar word—*amrita*—is used for the food of the Hindu gods, and the most probable explanation is that both ambrosia and nectar are forms of honey. The drink of the gods, therefore, was mead, an ancient alcoholic drink made from honey fermented with water and yeast, and frequently flavored with fruits and herbs or secondarily fermented with raisins. Mead has been around for at least three thousand years: Pliny and Aristotle both discuss it (Pliny called it *militites* and differentiated it from honey-sweetened wine),

and Anglo-Saxon heroes drank and roared in the mead hall. Though largely obliterated in modern Europe by wine and beer, it has ironically returned to public consciousness—at least in certain quarters—by its reappearance as the drink of choice in Dungeons & Dragons games, pseudo-medieval fantasy fiction, and the many computer games that echo the genre.

Curiously, some sources won't have it. In this translation by James Davidson, Hermippus, the one-eyed Athenian comedy writer of the fifth century BC, has the god Dionysos talking about wine, including the Mendaean wine,

with which the gods themselves wet their soft beds. And then there is Magnesian, generous, sweet and smooth, and Thasian upon whose surface skates the perfume of apples; this I judge by far the best of all the wines, except for blameless, painless Chian.

This last suggests that even Dionysos himself, the god of wine, was not immune to hangovers.

Did Clarence really drown in a butt of malmsey?

ACCORDING to Shakespeare's *Tragedy of Richard III*, Act I, Scene IV, George Plantagenet, Duke of Clarence, brother of King Edward IV and of the soon-to-be King Richard III, is murdered in the Tower of London in the following manner:

SECOND MURDERER: . . . Come, shall we fall to work?

FIRST MURDERER: Take him on the costard [head] with the hilts of thy sword, and then chop him in the malmsey-butt in the next room.

SECOND MURDERER: O excellent device! and make a sop of him.

[. . .]

SECOND MURDERER: Look behind you, my lord.

FIRST MURDERER: (*Stabbing him.*) Take that, and that. If all this will not do, I'll drown you in the malmsey-butt within.

(*Exits with the body.*)

The Duke of Clarence, age twenty-nine when he died, was a turbulent, treasonous nuisance. Shakespeare has him dream, on the night before he was killed, about drowning in the sea (prescience!) and going to Hell, where the ghost of a man he had killed at the Battle of Tewkesbury calls him "false, fleeting, perjur'd Clarence." He had joined with his father-in-law, the Earl of Warwick, the most powerful man in England save the king, in attempting to overthrow his brother King Edward IV, imprisoning Edward and executing Edward's father-in-law and brother-in-law. Although forgiven by Edward, Clarence continued to involve himself in other plots and conspiracies during the Wars of the Roses, always hoping to supplant him as king. He was arrogant and unstable, wholly lacking in political skills, and full of wild talk. By 1477, he was morbidly—some say paranoically—suspicious, convinced that Edward wanted him murdered. He even burst into a session of the Privy Council, shouting wild accusations against some of Edward's followers. Edward had had

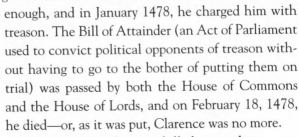

enough, and in January 1478, he charged him with treason. The Bill of Attainder (an Act of Parliament used to convict political opponents of treason without having to go to the bother of putting them on trial) was passed by both the House of Commons and the House of Lords, and on February 18, 1478, he died—or, as it was put, Clarence was no more.

The story that he was killed as tradition says has some contemporary support. Dominico Mancini, an Italian scholar who visited England from about late 1482 until just before Richard's coronation, wrote five years after the event that Clarence was "plunged into a jar of sweet wine"; Philippe de Commynes wrote in his *Mémoires* fewer than ten years later that "*Le roy Edouard fist mourir son frère, duc de Clarance, en un pippe de malvoisie, pour ce qu-il se vouloit faire roy, comme l'on disoit.*" Furthermore, he says that Clarence was invited to choose the manner of his death, and he chose to be drowned in a butt of malmsey. On the other hand, Shakespeare has him stabbed, which does not appear in his historical sources, so perhaps he at least did not entirely believe the tale.

When we think of malmsey now, we think of madeira wine, but for Shakespeare this was not the case. The island itself was only discovered in the fourteenth century, and it was only near the end of the sixteenth century that a wine industry was fully established. The term, in fact, was used for a range of unusually rich, sweet, long-lasting white wines produced in Greece, on the Ionian Islands, and on some of the Cyclades, but especially on Crete (then called Candia), which was the source of the best and most luxurious malmsey wine. The name *malmsey* is actually a corruption of the word *Malvasia* (*malvoisie* in French, as per Commynes), the name of the grape, and did not refer to a specific wine; rather, it denoted any strong, sweet wine from Greece and the islands of the eastern Mediterranean. The size of a butt was also different from the modern equivalent: while today it is 172 gallons, in 1483 a butt held only 108 gallons, but this was still large enough to drown a man.

Many modern historians think that the whole story is ridiculous, and tend to restrict themselves to remarking that Clarence had been condemned to death and died in the Tower. There is the possibility, however, that at least part of the story is correct: that he died in a butt of liquid, but that it was not malmsey. This was the argument put by John Webster Spargo in an academic article some three-quarters of a century ago. Because historians over the years appear to have assumed that this was a method of execution known nowhere else, it therefore could not be authentic: rather, it was merely a jest. However, Webster argues that in the Netherlands, there were examples of those charged with heresy being drowned in a vessel of water. He then cites a business letter written in 1479 as evidence that malmsey was common in London at the time, and thus the presence of a large wine barrel in the area of the Tower that housed noble prisoners also would have been common. (It was the merchants of Venice who created the demand for malmsey in England.) But what was in the barrel? Webster argues that "if the butt had still contained wine at the time of the execution, it would not have been available for occupancy by Clarence, for the head of the barrel would still have been intact." His conclusion was that it was an old malmsey butt, which, still having a capital value, had had its head knocked out and been filled with water to keep it from drying out. There is an additional argument against death by sweet wine: both murderers refer to a malmsey-butt, not a butt of malmsey—and there is a distinct difference between a water bucket and a bucket of water.

We shall, of course, never know for sure, but what is certain is that the First Murderer's announcing to Clarence that "I'll drown you in the water-butt within" would not have quite the same romantic resonance.

Can anyone remember why we drink to forget?

THAT REMINDS US of the one where this guy is getting plastered in a bar and the barman says, "You've had enough, pal," and the guy says, "No, no, you can't do this to me, I'm drinking to forget," and the barman says, "Forget what?" and the guy thinks for a bit and says, "I can't remember."

That reminds me of the one . . . The cry of the barroom bore throughout history. But there's some truth in the joke: we do try to drown our sorrows in wine. Alas, there is also some falsehood in the joke, because—as anyone who has lived with a drinker knows—it simply doesn't work. After a while, even the most hardened drunk becomes maudlin. Color, bouquet, taste, finish—all are subsumed in an onrush of terrible *remembering*, as grievances and hurts bubble to the surface on a tide of tears.

The drunk never remembers anything new to be sorrowful about. The reminiscences seldom vary: his mother was cruel to him, his father abandoned him, his wife had an affair, he was bullied at school and unappreciated at work. All are legitimate sadnesses, but through the refracting glass of wine they are magnified, rehearsed, and magnified again. We may drink to forget, but what we forget is . . . how to forget.

And now science has come out in support of the terrible memoriousness of the drunk. An article published in the *Journal of Neuroscience* in 2007 declared that moderate amounts of alcohol offer the brain a challenge to which it responds by improving memory.

But one has to judge intake carefully. One of the article's authors, Professor Matthew During of the University of Auckland, told the *Daily Telegraph* that "contrary to popular belief, our work suggests that heavy drinking actually reinforces negative memories."

Which still doesn't explain why it also makes the opposite sex look so very much more attractive.

When is antifreeze a bad thing?

FOR SEVERAL YEARS in the early 1980s, there was a run of high-yielding harvests in Austria. This increase in the quantity of grapes was a real threat to the wine industry, because the grapes made thin, acidic wine. Unfortunately, the overwhelming proportion was bulk wine produced for German supermarkets and other large consumer outlets, and they wanted what their customers wanted: cheap, medium-sweet wine. In desperation, many of the brokers dependent on that market decided to sweeten the wine. The problem was, sugar could be detected, so, reportedly on the advice of a wine consultant, the bulk wine producers added diethylene glycol, whose primary use, it was said, was as a component of antifreeze for automobiles. It was indeed not detected. What broke the scandal was the attempt of one producer to claim the cost of the diethylene glycol as a business expense on his tax return.

The result was utter disaster. The Austrian government announced that about 300,000 liters of the wine had been shipped to Germany, but then it was discovered that in the city of Cologne alone, 490,000 bottles of tainted wine had been impounded. German orders were canceled. The U.S. Bureau of Alcohol, Tobacco, and Firearms announced that twelve brands of wines imported from Austria had been found to be contaminated, and they advised consumers to drink no Austrian wines at all until all had been tested. As some hundreds of Austrian wines were imported into the United States, this was expected to take some time. Adulterated wine was also discovered in the Netherlands, France, Britain, Switzerland, and Poland. Matters were not helped when it was revealed that a Beerenauslese that had won a gold medal the previous year had been dosed to increase its body and sweetness. Austrian wine exports virtually ceased. The small village of Rust in Burgenland hung a banner over the highway proclaiming that it was "the prettiest wine-growing town in Austria—with unadulterated wine." Nevertheless, a Ruster Beerenauslese 1983 was found to have been adulterated.

Nor was it the Austrian government's finest hour: they had waited for three months after the discovery before warning the public. They were then forced to react by the furor. It was reported that at least thirty-eight companies were involved, and, fairly rapidly, two of the men involved found themselves in jail. Of more permanent benefit, Austria passed what are possibly the strictest wine laws in the world, which carry significant penalties for those who break them.

Many Austrian producers, as well as those who drink Austrian wine, now believe that the scandal was the best thing that could have happened to the industry. Many middlemen were forced out of business, and the producers therefore had to deal directly with customers themselves—and this encouraged the production of better wines. This was helped by a generational change, as younger winemakers, many familiar with the wine world outside of Austria, succeeded to positions of responsibility. The watchword became quality, with the result that Austrian wines today can hold their own with some of the best in the world.

There is an irony in all of this. It was probably the case that the scandal fed on what was an easily understood threat: drinking antifreeze. In fact, most antifreezes consist mainly of ethylene glycol, *not* diethylene glycol: diethylene glycol would only be half as good in preventing your car's radiator from freezing up. Therefore, what was added to the wine may not have been nice, but it was not antifreeze. This simple misconception probably

reflects the regrettable lack by most journalists of a basic knowledge of chemistry.

Care for some Gevrey-Chambertin with those organ pipes?

THE MONASTIC PROFESSION has always been curiously competitive, and nowhere more so than in Ottobeuren, just thirty miles
as the crow flies from Weingarten (see p. 39) and the birthplace,
in 1710, of Karl Josef Riepp. On the death of their father, Riepp
and his brother Rupert moved to Strasbourg to learn organ
building with the great André Silbermann. In 1741, Riepp married a woman from Dole, formerly capital of Franche-Comté in
the Saône Valley, before settling in Dijon. Not content with
confining himself to organ building, Riepp was admitted to the
wine merchants' corporation of Dijon in 1748.

Twelve years later, the monks of Ottobeuren decided to commission a new organ for their new basilica—and one that would
outshine Gabler's instrument at Weingarten. Despite Gabler's
having enrolled his son as a novice in the Ottobeuren monastery,
word of the chaos of the Weingarten contract had reached the
monks' ears. Riepp put in a bid; not only was he an Ottobeuren
man, but he was also, unlike Gabler, actually an organ builder. It
was time for the return of the native: Karl Josef Riepp got the
contract.

Promising the monks a fine instrument in the new German
style, Riepp nevertheless delivered, between 1761 and 1766, a
tremendous, powerful, and magnificent instrument in what was
unmistakably the *French* style. The monks of Ottobeuren didn't
complain, for every time Riepp sent a consignment of organ pipes
up from Dijon, he included a few "sample" cases of his wines; by
then, he was no longer just a merchant, but owned vineyards in
Vosne-Romanée and Gevrey-Chambertin, and his vintages were
gaining a reputation for themselves.

Predictably, the "samples" produced firm orders in return, and—despite Riepp's declaration that "if there are better organs in Europe, then my name's Jack"—it seems that he made more money on the wine than he did from the organ.

Karl Josef Riepp died in Dijon on May 5, 1775, leaving a certain degree of financial confusion and some noble vineyards to his wife, Anne-Françoise, and some equally noble organs to posterity. And, of course, some very happy monks.

Did Slovenia turn the British into a nation of wine drinkers?

IN THE NINETEENTH CENTURY, the Germans referred to England as the land *ohne Musik* (without music); it could certainly be argued that, at least until the 1970s and 1980s, Britain was the land *ohne Wein*. This is not, of course, to say that wine was not drunk; rather, beer was the usual drink, supplemented by gin. A special occasion might call for champagne; Christmas certainly called for a glass of (usually sweet) sherry. But as for wine's making a regular appearance with meals, this was relatively rare, even among the upper-middle and upper classes, the traditional buyers and drinkers of wines.

The Second World War appears to have changed this. Many Britons spent at least part of the war in France and, especially, Italy, where the south was occupied by the British and American armies from 1943. Many soldiers there discovered the regular—and for those countries, normal—pleasures of a glass of wine with their meals or over conversation with friends, and when they returned home, they wanted to continue this new way of life. But what to drink? Fortunately, Slovenia came to the rescue and provided a wine that took the new drinking classes by storm, becoming the best-selling white wine for several decades. This was Lutomer "Riesling."

This wine came from the region of Podravja, and the actual

grape is the Laski Rizling—the Germans were outraged at the theft of the name of their revered grape, and forced the Slovenians to change it and use its proper name. The grape must (juice) was fermented at the winery, shipped in bulk to Ljubljana, substantially sweetened with unfermented grape juice (*süssreserve*) and perhaps some extra sugar, fortified with sulfur to keep it from going off, shipped in tankers to the London docks, stored, and bottled as needed. Britain became awash with medium-sweet white wine. It went down easily, it was cheap, and it gave an added touch of sophistication to many British households. Everyone needs a starter wine—few are born preferring a *grand cru* claret or an acidic muscadet—and for many Britons, Lutomer provided it. Most went on to develop a taste for dryer wines. But there was one regrettable result, which was that a liking for sweet white wines, whatever the quality, is now often perceived as the mark of a person who lacks sophistication, and who certainly knows nothing about wine (except that she knows what she likes).

Does the wine of Antipaxos exist?

H. G. WELLS wrote a story called "The Magic Shop" that is centered upon, not surprisingly, a magic shop. His narrator finds it on London's Regent Street, although "I had fancied it was down nearer the Circus, or round the corner in Oxford Street, or even in Holborn; always over the way and a little inaccessible it had been, with something of the mirage in its position."

There are wines like that, and perhaps the wine most like that is the fabled wine of Antipaxos. Trawl the Internet, rummage through the books, and you will find numerous references to it . . . but all of them different, always over the way and a little inaccessible. Some say it is light and white and fragrant, others that it is rich and red; some say you will occasionally find it for sale, others that it is *never* sold, but kept—it is made in tiny quantities, of course—for the families who make it. Occasionally a writer who has fallen under the spell will recount the tale of a taverna owner who takes a particular liking to him or her ("I  felt that Tassos and I had become firm friends") and produces an unlabeled bottle from some secret recess that transports them into a strange and hazily contemplative mood as they stumble home through the olive groves . . .

Well, Antipaxos itself exists, for sure, a mile or so south of the tiny Ionian island of Paxos. Paxos itself is an odd place: legend has it that a ship, piloted by one Thamus, was sailing from Italy to Greece, and as it passed the Paxos shoreline, a voice cried out, "Thamus, when you get to Palodes, be sure to proclaim that the great god Pan is dead."

And Antipaxos is a mere speck in comparison.

But we have had the Antipaxos wine and can solve the mystery. The wine of Antipaxos is a slightly sweet, quite heavy white wine, light red in color, a bit like a Beaujolais; it's notably heavy and alcoholic, quite chewy with tannin, while at the same time being dry and amber-yellow with a hint of eucalyptus and honey, dark, almost black, and heavily fruited with blackcurrant and raspberry.

In other words, it's any number of things. Each time, one is told that *this* is the genuine, the *only* Antipaxos wine, whether it's on sale in the bakery in Gaios, the tiny capital of the island, or produced by a local from the depths of his olive-oil warehouse in a plastic gas can, or materialized from the cellar of a Lakka taverna in an unlabeled bottle, or however it comes.

It is, in short, a mystery. For the wine bluffer, this is a godsend. If anyone speaks of the mysterious Antipaxos, you can simply say, "I know it well," and describe anything that comes into your head, secure in the knowledge that, at some time or other, someone will have drunk something called Antipaxos that is *exactly as you have described.* It is indeed a veritable Proteus of wines, a shape-shifter, an elusive reminder that some things are beyond our ken. It would, of course, be a simple matter to putter over to Antipaxos, climb the hill, and ask a few questions, but that, we feel, would somehow spoil it. Much better to let it remain as it is: wine's equivalent of the Magic Shop.

When should wine smell of petrol?

IT IS QUITE possible that relatively few people would respond favorably to an invitation to try a glass of wine because it has notes of petrol in the bouquet. The others would be foolish not to grab the glass. Petrol is a benchmark aroma identifying a good riesling with some age. Young European rieslings with any quality at all overwhelm the senses with aromas of flowers and often of lime; those from hotter climates may include tropical fruit in the list. But as they begin to age, they change. The flowers begin to develop into honey, and the notes of petrol emerge more and more. By the time a great German or Alsace riesling is, say, twenty years old—and riesling can age and age— the combination is quite sublime. Many wine drinkers have failed to grasp the pleasures they are missing. The result, for those of us who do, is that the wines can be wonderfully underpriced.

An omelette and a glass of wine?

THE QUESTION—sans question mark—comes from the great Elizabeth David's collection of cookery and food writing, published in 1984. It conjures an image of perfect simplicity and perfect eating and drinking. We can smell the lavender and the fig trees and feel the heat of the sun. And such perfection requires neither great expense nor great luxury, just attention to detail and the careful matching of ingredients.

Which is odd.

We know, almost certainly, the precise omelette Miss David had in mind. It was *l'omelette de la Mère Poulard*, as made by the proprietress of the Auberge de Saint-Michel Tête d'Or at Mont Saint-Michel, who died in 1931, age eighty, but not before revealing the "secret" of her celebrated omelettes:

Je casse de bons oeufs dans une terrine, je les bats bien, je mets un bon morceau de beurre dans le poêle, j'y jette les oeufs et je remue constamment.

Good eggs, bowl, mix, frying pan, butter, keep 'em moving . . . and that's that. So much for the omelette. Now: what about the glass of wine?

And here's the problem: it's an absolute given that two things that *never* go well together are wine and eggs.

Contemplate a boiled egg, buttered toast, and a glass of Brouilly, and your mental taste buds rise in rebellion. A Trockenbeerenauslese with two fried eggs? Oh dear. Scrambled eggs and a fair young Beaujolais? No. *No.* The palate quite correctly rejects the combination, and it is nothing to do with the choice of wine. *Any* wine will seem disgusting with eggs, and the taste of both will be ruined. True, there is a French dish, *oeufs à la meurette*, in which the eggs are poached with wine, but even Homer nods.

Why eggs and wine should not mix is unclear. We suspect sulfur has something to do with it; perhaps, too, that is why the humble (it has much to be humble about) Brussels sprout is also wine's enemy. As is that signifier of luxury, asparagus.

A shame. But the Brussels sprout, if you must, can be accompanied with a good Normandy cider with no loss of face to either; asparagus can be indulged in before the first wine is poured; and as for the omelette, Guinness Imperial Russian Stout carries away the laurels, lightly chilled on a hot day.

So what was Miss David thinking of?

We should remember that her first book was published in 1950, when Britain was still afflicted with postwar shortages, the hideous memory of snoek and Woolton pie still vivid. Food was fuel, not sensual pleasure, and pretty poor fuel, too. Even acknowledging the pleasures of the table was the first step to becoming a terrible garlic-smelling, tax-evading, siesta-taking foreigner.

Into this gray climate, Miss David brought not so much a recipe book as a glimpse of better things. What could be better, in a nation still reeling from powdered egg, than a perfect omelette? What better to take away the taste of sour, watery wartime beer than a glass of wine? And the combination of the two lit up the imagination, whether or not it worked in reality. After all, people dream happily of making love on a tropical beach, and thoughts of sunburn, insects, and all-pervading sand never enter their heads. Miss David was simply conjuring up a mood, and conjuring it beautifully.

Also, of course, the pleasures of the table, like all such delights, are as much enjoyed in anticipation as in reality. And we have to admit that, as a temptation to sensual speculation, *An Omelette and a Bottle of Stout* just somehow doesn't work.

How about a glass of fermented grape must?

ACCORDING TO THE European Union definition, "fermented grape must," no matter how unattractive it sounds, is wine. Grape must is what you get by crushing grapes; the word *must* derives from the Latin adjective *mustus*, meaning "fresh" or "new" (that is, the juice before fermenting it to make wine). The problem is that the English word *musty*, which is not derived from the Latin (it is probably derived from *moist*), means "moldy."

So long as the label says *wine* and doesn't refer to must, no one is going to be put off drinking the liquid in the bottle. However, those who choose to make very low-alcohol wines have a problem:

EU regulations. One Italian winemaker, by stopping the fermentation of the natural grape sugars long before they are all used up, produces an interesting sweet red wine with only 5 percent alcohol. Under the regulations, he's not allowed to call it wine, but he is allowed to use the word *must*. Therefore, he labels his wine *mosto parzialmente fermentato*, or "partially fermented must." Perhaps it sounds better in Italian.

Shall we have a glass of raisin juice?

THE CAREFUL READER of "Yes, but what exactly *is* wine?" will have noted that, according to European Union regulations, wine must be made from fresh grapes, which are defined as "fruit of the vine . . . ripe or even slightly raisined." This could be slightly confusing, since *raisins* in French just refers to grapes, while in English a raisin is a dried grape.

The method of drying grapes before crushing them to produce the juice or must that is fermented to make wine was practiced by the ancient Hittites and by the Greeks in the time of Homer. (The Hittites, who had a remarkable empire from about the seventeenth to the thirteenth century BC in what is now central Turkey, have regrettably faded from the group memory, unlike the Greeks. The first written diplomatic treaty that survives, which is inscribed on gold and which is an agreement to carve up Syria, was agreed between the Hittites and the Egyptians. Uriah the Hittite has a walk-on part in the Bible: coveting Uriah's wife, King David sent Uriah into battle and certain death.)

Nowadays, the three best-known wines made from grapes that have been dried are all Italian: Vin Santo from Tuscany, and Amarone and Recioto della Valpolicella from Veneto. The effect of the drying is to concentrate the natural sugars (glucose and fructose) before the fermentation is begun, which gives greater sweetness and/or alcoholic strength to the finished wine.

Amarone is a dry red wine that used to be prized by some drinkers for its high alcohol content, exceeding 15 percent (which is, unfortunately, not so unusual nowadays). Recioto della Valpolicella is a sweet red wine, notable for going very well with chocolate desserts.

Ceremonial: will you take wine?

IT IS IMPOSSIBLE to ascertain whether it was George Bernard Shaw or Oscar Wilde who first observed that Britain and America are two countries separated by a common language. Wilde uses the phrase in *The Canterville Ghost,* while a 1951 dictionary of quotations attributes something similar to Shaw, but without giving a specific reference.

But it's true, and also true that the two countries are separated by common customs. Take, for example, the oddly stilted but rather charming custom of "taking wine." We don't refer here to bringing a bottle of something nice along to a friend's house for dinner, but to the formal business conducted at Masonic guest nights, Rotary Club dinners, and so forth. Here's a Masonic version, from the United States:

> During dinner the Master of the Lodge MAY "Take Wine" in the English manner with various brothers. This action will be announced, and presided over by the Worshipful Brother who is serving as "Toast Master" or "Master of Ceremonies" at Table Proceedings. The announcement of wine-taking is made by the "Toast Master" in a single sentence, i.e.: "Brethren, the W.M. will take wine with his Wardens." Whereupon, the Master and the Brother(s) designated for the honor rise and the Master may make remarks recognizing the honoree(s), who then salute one another with their glasses and drink, then resume their seats. The Master may call on one of the honorees for his comments.

ONLY THOSE WHO ARE CALLED TO TAKE WINE WILL STAND.
THE REMAINDER OF THE COMPANY WILL REMAIN SEATED.

If the Toastmaster or the Master calls for the Brethren to take wine with a particular guest or other Companion, then ALL STAND. It is considered polite for short applause after each wine-taking.

Only a churl could take exception to this process, although it does seem a little elaborate. But the odd thing to an English eye is the phrase "in the English manner." We have indeed seen this done at formal English dinners, though only seldom, and the usual comment is that this must be an American custom that has found its way across the Atlantic, the Americans being less reticent about declarations of brotherhood (or sisterhood) than the British.

Whatever the case, we are glad to see it, and will happily "take wine" with anyone who cares to suggest it.

Is wine becoming more alcoholic?

WINE IS DEFINITELY more alcoholic than it used to be. The tendency toward a higher level of alcohol began with Californian, Australian, and other New World reds. In the introduction to his *Pocket Wine Book 2008*, Oz Clarke complains of winemakers "following the False High Priest of superripeness"—could this possibly be Robert Parker? (see p. 170)—and producing the consequent high alcohol levels. Even France has succumbed, he says. Red Bordeaux used to be 11.5 to 12.5 percent alcohol, and now there are wines over 14.5 percent alcohol. Too much alcohol for a particular wine style spoils the taste and makes it hard to enjoy more than a glass.

The British government is becoming concerned about problem drinking in the middle classes. They are increasing their alcohol intake, which, given the increasingly high levels of alcohol, rises even if the volume of wine they consume does not increase. In a rather obscure effort to deal with this, London is urging the EU to make it easier to sell wines with an alcohol level as low as 6.5 percent. Ridiculously, the British Food Standards Agency has in recent years had to impound low-alcohol wines in order to comply with EU rules.

If you don't want to wait for the EU regulations to be changed, try some older German rieslings, which should be well below 10 percent alcohol.

What was all that about Mateus Rosé?

HOW IS IT that some wines simply sum up a specific period? For 1960s Britain, it was probably Blue Nun Liebfraumilch (see p. 104) or perhaps Bull's Blood. For America in the same period, Thunderbird and Lancers spring to mind. In the 1970s, after a heated race between them, Mateus Rosé won the day. The very name, to those who were alive then, conjures up images of the inevitable steakhouse—in all probability, Britain's long-gone Berni Inns chain—with shrimp cocktail to start, then a rump steak with "all the trimmings" (an entirely flavorless tomato, half a dozen pallid button mushrooms fresh from the can, and rehydrated dehydrated catering "peas"), concluding with Black Forest Gâteau and a "specialty coffee," usually called "Irish," which meant the sort of coffee that today would make even a trainee barista faint with horror, laced with whisky, and topped with a strange, slimy layer of floating cream. All "washed down"—that was the phrase they used—with a bottle of Mateus Rosé.

It was a masterpiece of wine branding: the characteristic squat bottle, the picture of the elegant castle on the label, the sweetish inoffensiveness of the vaguely *pétillant* wine inside. It went perfectly with the entire repertoire of British middle-of-the-market dining out, from A to B, and was somehow redolent of flared trousers, mushroom-brown polyester safari jackets, Hush Puppies shoes, and round-collared jersey-knit patterned shirts. If you inhaled deeply, you could almost smell the memory of patchouli.

For many of us, Mateus Rosé was last seen being wielded by the ghost of Manuel in a sort of revenant *Fawlty Towers*, where the Dining Experience was summed up, in one episode, by a man trying to change his dinner order only to be told by Sybil, "I'm afraid it's a bit late; chef *has* opened the *tin*." We moved on, and Mateus Rosé (one *always* mentioned the Rosé part, as if there were many other forms of Mateus to choose from) stayed behind.

For the economist, influential blogger, and self-confessed head of the shadowy international scandium oligopoly Tim Worstall, who lives in Lisbon, Mateus never went away:

It's simply one brand of the rosé version of one of the great Portuguese traditions, *vinho verde*, meaning green wine, or young wine. White, red, rosé, dry, semi-dry (and very rarely, sweetish), great racks of the supermarket shelves are taken up with it . . . and, yes, the Portuguese really do buy it. It isn't just some crud whipped up to sell to the ignorant Brits.

Not that we wish to accuse Worstall of being disingenuous or overloyal to his adopted country, but there is a little more to it than that. The truth is that Mateus Rosé is almost entirely the creation of a marketing genius, Fernando van Zeller Guedes, who founded the Sociedade Comercial dos Grandes Vinhos de Mesa de Portugal in 1942 (now in third-generation family ownership and known as SOGRAPE Vinhos SA). What Guedes was after was a wine with a clearly Portuguese identity but which would appeal to an international—and not necessarily wine-drinking—market. He was, in a sense, trying to scoop up the beer drinkers from one side and the soda drinkers from the other. And he succeeded. Mateus Rosé achieved an almost unheard-of brand recognition, and this before the days of sophisticated demographics, computerized market research, or any of the other tricks of twenty-first-century branding.

What he did have (apart from a fairly average *vinho verde* made from red Douro varietals such as Baga, Tinta Barroca and Rufete) was *image*. The bottle—lifted from the traditional Franconian *Bocksbeutel*—was simultaneously unlike any other mass-market wine bottle, but with the odd familiarity of the military water canteen. As for the label, it does indeed show the Casa de Mateus, but the stuff has never been made there. The current count's grandmother made a shrewd deal with Guedes, allowing him to use the Casa on his label in return for a supply of grapes for fermentation and resale, an agreement that lasted until Portugal's April Revolution of 1974.

But like all brands unless carefully nurtured, Mateus Rosé fell into the abyss of unfashionability. For anyone passing as a sophisticate in the 1980s, to order—or even acknowledge the existence of—Mateus meant instant loss of credibility. A publican in the family told us that he had visited the Mateus winery. "Not to buy," he said hurriedly, "just to see. And what I saw . . . I made a solemn vow I would *never speak of it*." Pure bravado, of course, but it showed how déclassé Mateus Rosé had become. The wine remained the same, but the image had failed.

And there was worse to come. On the *Whisky Magazine* Web site for December 26, 2006, one "daisy12chic" posted a message headed "Mateus Rose" (*sic*), whose text would have made Guedes's hair stand on end. "We have a bottle," the message read. "I am including the image. Not sure what it is—might be wine. Thanks!"

How are the mighty fallen. Yet the company is not giving up the struggle. The Mateus Rosé has been reformulated, the bottle redesigned, and other wines—an Aragonês, a Shiraz, a Tempranillo, and an unspecified Mateus White—have been added to the range.

Who knows—in a world exhausted by intricate televisual gastronomy, where even Delia Smith has now written a book on how to cheat at cooking, the 1970s may yet return to our dinner tables, and Mateus may once again come to symbolize the good life.

Is English wine any good?

THE ANSWER TO this question is yes—and some of it is very good. It is primarily white and sparkling, and there is not very much of it. England and Wales have fewer than 3 square miles of vines for winemaking. Even in England, only a minuscule proportion of the wines on sale are English, and outside of England, you are likely to encounter English wines only when you attend a reception at your local British embassy.

The relatively cool English climate and its often cloudy weather are the reasons for the skepticism implied by the question. Winemaking in the world is largely confined to two belts: from 30° to 50° north of the Equator and from 30° to 50° south: beyond 50° north and south, it is too cold for grapes to ripen, while in the reaches between 30° north and south, there is no cold season to allow the vines to rest. Only the tiniest bit of England, the tip of the Lizard Peninsula in Cornwall, just scrapes into the vine-growing belt. Yet the temperature is not the most crucial consideration; rather, it is sunshine. Vines normally require a minimum of 1,500 hours of sunshine, with more needed by red than by white grapes. One drawback to growing vines in England is immediately obvious. The other is the propensity to rain *all year*, in contrast, for example, to the Mediterranean or California, where there are wet seasons and dry seasons. The dry, sunny weather before the grape harvest that is characteristic of those two areas is a gift to winemakers: the weather concentrates the sugars in the grapes, and the subsequent fermentation converts the sugars into a high level of alcohol. A lack of sunny weather means a lack of sugars and a high level of acidity. Too much rain fosters disastrous rots, and if by some dispensation from heaven rot is held at bay, the vines will suck up the rainwater and thereby dilute the grape juice.

Nevertheless, time and again attempts have been made to grow grapes. First came the Romans, who invaded, first in 55 BC and again in AD 43, conquered, and held England for three centuries. They planted vines, possibly for winemaking (opinions differ). In any case, whether they produced it or imported it, they left many Britons with the habit of drinking wine. Later, the influence of the Church was crucial, because all institutions from tiny parish churches to great monasteries required wine for communion. This cultivation of vines was facilitated by the warming of the northern European climate for eight centuries until the mid-thirteenth century, when it began to cool, thereby worsening the conditions for growing grapes. A century later, the Black Death (1348–49) wiped out one-third of the population of Europe, which meant that abbeys and monasteries no longer had access to the necessary labor to continue to cultivate all of their own land, and increasingly leased it out. Tenants wanted to produce fast-growing cash crops, not vines that needed tending for years, and vineyards were grubbed up. King Henry VIII's dissolution of the monasteries in the 1530s, which saw the land and buildings sold off or given away, condemned most of the remaining vineyards and ended winemaking on any scale in England. By the late seventeenth century, when the climate had become considerably colder, the diarist Samuel Pepys described the few English vineyards as "brave plantations."

By the early twentieth century, the commercial growing of grapes for wine in England had virtually disappeared. The man responsible for the new dawn was Ray Barrington Brock, managing director of a firm of scientific instrument makers, who was a keen gardener and who saw the growing of grapes as a challenge. The overall question was how to grow grapes in a cool—and relatively wet—climate. In 1945, Brock founded the Oxted Viticultural Research Station (he lived in Oxted, Surrey), the first part of which was established in his own garden, and there for the next quarter century he experimented with hundreds of varieties of grapevine, most of which were failures in the English climate. He funded all of this himself, partly by the sale of vine cuttings and the books and pamphlets he wrote on the subject, but primarily from the profits of his main business, having remained in full employment during his years of research. For fifteen years he was able to offset the expenses of the research station against his other income, but in 1960 the tax inspector decided that it would never make a profit and was therefore not a business that could attract tax relief. Brock's devotion to the cause and his financial sacrifices earned him two enduring rewards: the Jones-Bateman Cup for original research into fruit culture from the Royal Horticultural Society, and a position in history as the founding father of the British commercial wine industry.

A beneficiary of Brock's work was Sir Guy Salisbury-Jones, GCVO, CMG, MC, DL, the first man in the twentieth century to plant a vineyard in England with the intention of making wine for sale on a commercial basis. It was established in the winter of 1951 at Hambledon in Hampshire, and four years later the first bottles went on sale, a fact that caused a small media frenzy. Salisbury-Jones himself was an asset in awakening the public to English wine: he was tall and imposing, had had a distinguished, if sometimes colorful, military and diplomatic career, and was a notable presence in any assembly. His wines improved markedly over the years and sold widely, and Hambledon became one of the first English vineyards to export wine to the United States.

There are now many small and medium-sized wineries in England and Wales. Although some growers persist with red wine grapes, most of the wine produced is white. The glory of English wine, however, is sparkling wine, at least two of which are of international standard. Global warming, while not precisely providing the south coast of England with a Mediterranean climate, has nevertheless made it easier to grow grapes. Indeed, the climate in Sussex, home of the best of these wines, is not so far removed from that of the Champagne region of France a century ago. Sussex also has a similar *terroir* (see p. 15), sharing the chalk-based soil that runs from Champagne through the White Cliffs of Dover to Sussex. Indeed, there are repeated reports of French champagne firms sniffing around Sussex for possible purchases of land, which, as expensive as land is in England, is spectacularly less so than land in Champagne.

In short, while there is in England, as in all winemaking countries, wine that is merely drinkable, a decent amount of English white wine is very good—and many of the sparkling wines are excellent.

Glass of prewar lemonade, chaps?

JAMES BIGGLESWORTH—"Biggles"—was (or is) the fictional First World War fighter ace who stars in the stories by Captain W. E. Johns and upon whom Snoopy, the beagle fantasist in the *Peanuts* strip, models himself when seated on the doghouse roof, scarf magically blown back in the nonexistent slipstream as he narrates his own adventures to himself ("Here's the famous World War One fighter ace . . .").

Biggles is presented as an inspiring leader of men, a red-hot pilot, and a man of fierce loyalties, given to the red mist descending over his eyes in the face of injustice, but otherwise the *preux chevalier*, a warrior of honor. The First World War books reflect, accurately in many ways, the realities of life for a British pilot in France—not least the remarkable unpreparedness of the new aircrew for active service (some arrived in France after a mere 17.5 hours of flight training) and their appalling life expectancy of, on average, just a couple of months.

But in one significant way, Biggles is different. After a particularly grueling mission, he is prone to announce to his fellow pilots that he's off into town, where he's heard there's a place where you can still get prewar lemonade. His squadron competes with others for a case of lemonade donated by a colonel. Lemonade is Biggles's drink of choice. *Lemonade?* In *France?* Among the notoriously hard-drinking, dangerous-living fighter pilots? Surely not.

Nor was it, indeed. The great prize in France at the time was wine, and for "prewar lemonade" we should read "pre-phylloxera wine." Literally. W. E. Johns's publishers had decided that wine drinking set the wrong example, and told Johns so. Like anyone who enjoys a glass or two, Johns took this glumly, and responded simply by changing every reference to "wine" to "lemonade."

So Biggles was really one of us, after all.

Would this be the *vin du pays*?

ONE THING we don't hear much about these days is whether or not a particular wine "travels well." There was a time when some antipodean wines had a reputation for being a bit sketchy in that regard, but it was nothing to do with traveling well or badly; it was simply that as many as one in twelve bottles was corked. The explanation was that, in a sense, it was the *corks* that didn't travel well; being furthest from Portugal, the New Zealanders were paying the price. So they changed over en masse to screw caps, and the problem was solved.

It's easy to see why wine's tolerance of travel was once an issue. When southern French wines were shipped out of Toulon their journey could be hazardous beyond just the inconveniences of poor winds, high seas, dismasting, and bilge-polluted barrels; there were the frequently war-afflicted Straits of Gibraltar to contend with, and then the notorious Bay of Biscay, through which consignments from Portugal also had to pass.

Add to that the perils of lurching oxcarts, careless stevedores, rutted roads, perilous mountain passes, and all the heartaches and the thousand natural shocks that wine is heir to, and one can see how the question arose, particularly in Britain, where there was precious little *vin du pays* available.

Now, of course, things are different. Fast, smooth container ships, speedy road transport, bottling on site or shipping in stainless-steel vessels, temperature-controlled transport, and, of course, the expensive but stress-free air transport (for ordinary freight, not "self-loading freight," as the airline industry refers to passengers): all these have rendered wine's voyage from its birthplace to the table infinitely less fraught.

Yet we should not forget the psychological perils of traveling wine. That crisply volcanic Greco di Tufo that so coolly charmed the palate in the little restaurant off the via Monserrato seems pale and thin back in Manchesters England and New Hampshire alike; the enchantingly idiosyncratic Antipaxos wine (see p. 117, and depending which version you got) so redolent of the wine-dark Ionian does not send your guests back in Düsseldorf or Melbourne into *quite* the rhapsodies you expected. The delights of the *vin* so often require the presence of the *pays*.

And even that does not always work. The historian, Arabist, author, traveler, wine connoisseur, and bon vivant Raymond Flower is the sort of figure England once exported around the world. Now there are sadly few of him, and none who could, as he legendarily (or perhaps mythically) did, spend a year living at the Palace Hotel, St. Moritz, to write a book about it.

Flower's place in the oenophiles' hall of fame rests on his book

Chianti, a history of the region largely told through wine. But his place in Valhalla itself is ensured by a story we heard from his own lips many years ago, at his adopted home in a medieval *torre* in Tuscany.

He was being visited (he recounted) by the late Marika Hanbury-Tenison, gastronome, food editor, and cookery editor of the London *Daily Telegraph*. It can, even for so accomplished a host as Flower, be a nerve-racking business entertaining such a one at dinner, so, he said, he laid it on a bit.

Sitting on the terrace of his house, which stands, like all such ancient fortified buildings, on a small hill, with the Chianti dusk falling gently and the scent of his lemon trees on the air, he filled her glass.

"This," he said, "is my own wine."

"Is it, Raymond?" said Mrs. Hanbury-Tenison. "In what sense?"

"Made from my own grapes," he replied.

"And where are your vines?"

Raymond Flower gestured modestly down the hill beyond the dusty lane and across to where the land rose again.

"There," he said. "Not two hundred yards from where we are sitting."

She raised the glass to the light; swirled; inhaled; tasted.

"Really," she said. "Two hundred yards?" A gleam of pure and joyful mischief came into her eye. "Doesn't travel very well, does it?"

Is there still a place for feet in winemaking?

IN OLDEN TIMES, grapes were crushed by foot; there are masses of illuminated manuscripts and tapestries showing the *vendange* or harvest, with people treading grapes in round wooden tubs. Alas for tradition, there are very few places left in which this occurs. There are small producers in Burgundy, the Loire, Germany, Languedoc, and Rioja that do, and biodynamic producers are sometimes tempted and occasionally succumb, but the only serious treading for commercial production takes place in the Douro in Portugal. More than tradition is involved, however: it is actually the best way of crushing the grapes for premium port.

For port, the grape must, or juice, is fermented for only two days, at which point grape spirit (*aguardente*) is added to stop the fermentation while there is still a lot of sugar present in the must. (According to Maurice Healy in *Stay Me with Flagons*, the 1897 Sandeman vintage port was fortified with Scotch whisky.) This means that the must spends a much shorter time in contact with the skins than is normal for red wines—ten days for a fine red Bordeaux but no more than forty-eight hours for a port—and because this is the period when the color, tannins, and flavor compounds leach from the skins into the must, the maceration process must be as vigorous as possible.

Until the 1960s, every farm in the Douro had a winery equipped with a *lagar*, usually built from granite, which was about two feet deep and anywhere from ten to thirty feet square. This is where the grapes were crushed and the fermentation took place. At those farms where *lagares* are still used, the process is fundamentally the same. The *lagar* is filled over the course of a day by pickers dumping their baskets of grapes into it to within about ten or so inches from the brim, although at some places they might go through a hand-turned roller-crusher first. The grapes are then trodden by the vintagers. The human foot is ideal for pressing grapes, because it breaks them up without crushing the pips, which would release bitter flavor compounds into the must. The number of men is also important, because fermentation can be hastened or retarded by the heat of their bodies helping the working of the yeasts. Ideally, there should be two men per pipe (2,180 gallons).

A good tread results in a deeply colored must, with fermentation beginning at the outset, not, as with red wine, after the crushing of the grapes is finished. To ensure this, the treading is done in stages. First comes the cut or *corte*. The men line up in three or four rows, shoulder to shoulder, and with arms linked. They march on the spot, while the man in charge of the group of pickers sets the rhythm by shouting "one-two" or "left-right," their feet crushing the grapes against the stone floor of the *lagar*. This is dead monotonous. Periodically, the lines will move one step backward or forward in order to crush a new set of grapes. This goes on for two, or more likely three, hours. Then, at about 10 P.M., *liberdade* (freedom) is declared, with cups of *aguardente* and cigarettes handed out. Treading is continued, but now to the accompaniment of an accordion (real or recorded), or a drum, or a local group providing folk tunes. Depending on the amount of *aguardente* drunk, the treading can become quite lively, and certainly the treaders in their shorts will have purple pulp up to their thighs. This dancing around has a purpose beyond indulging high spirits: whole grapes are colder than the must, and often in corners, but also elsewhere, the dancing feet discover untrodden grapes. It all ends about midnight, by which time there should be no whole grapes left, just a mass of broken skins and juice. Traditionally, the test of the completeness of the extraction was to pour a little of the juice across a white plate: if it left behind a streaky red stain, it was enough.

Yeast is seldom added, because the ambient yeasts from the outsides of the skins of the grapes themselves will begin the fermentation by working on the sugar. By morning, the skins will have floated to the surface, and as fermentation progresses, a "cap" or crust will form. Planks are laid across the *lagar*, and men with special poles called *macacos* will push the cap below the surface until the desired color and sugar levels are reached. The juice is then run off the *lagar* into a vat that is already one-fifth full of *aguardente*, whose alcohol content is normally about

77 percent. When the two are mixed together, the yeasts are killed and the fermentation stopped. The maturing process then begins.

The use of feet rather than crushing machines results in port of a much higher quality, because, as noted above, feet ensure a higher extraction of the color, tannins, and flavor compounds without the danger of crushing the pips. The problem is that it is a very labor-intensive process. During the 1970s, the local youth began to leave the area: many of the young men were sent to fight Portugal's colonial wars in Mozambique and Angola, and both sexes went to the cities, where both job opportunities with much higher pay and excitement were in much greater supply than in the villages of the Douro. As a consequence, in the 1990s, many of the port producers began to bring in machines to supply the labor that humans were increasingly less willing to provide. Only the truly premium ports are now the result of feet.

Why did native American wine grapes make such bad wine?

WHEN THE FIRST colonists came to eastern North America in the early seventeenth century, they found masses of grapevines crawling up trees, snaking along the ground, and forming thick natural hedges. Grapevines meant wine, and wine meant that the colonists would not have to drink water, a liquid well known to cause illness and even death. In England, there was beer and ale, but in order to plant barley and hops, you needed what was then unavailable: a strong plow and oxen to pull it. Therefore, wine it would be. The first Englishmen emigrated to Virginia in 1607, but they did not seriously attempt to make wine in any quantity for some years, in spite of the urgings of the London shareholders in the enterprise, who were keen that wine should be made and exported from America. They wanted to make money from their investment in the colony, which, they thought, provided the right conditions for growing wine grapes. Furthermore, if the English wanted wine, they had to import it, and it was preferable that this money be kept within the empire, rather than going to those enemies of England who made wine. The Virginians sent a shipment of wine to London in 1622, but it spoiled en route and was unsaleable, and that ended that venture. In Massachusetts, the first Puritans emigrated in 1630, and tried to make wine during their first year. The result was so dire that they petitioned London to send out some French winemakers to show them how to do it. But if their winemaking was at fault, even more so were the grapes.

For winemaking, the best species is *Vitis vinifera*, which today is used for 99 percent of all of the wine consumed in the world. However, *V. vinifera* was not native to eastern North America, and when attempts were made in the eighteenth century to import cuttings and grow it in the colonies, the vines were destroyed by the significant variations in climate of the northeastern seaboard or by diseases such as phylloxera, to which native American varieties were largely immune. The most important native grapes were *Vitis labrusca*, *V. riparia*, and *V. rupestris*. *V. riparia* has often provided the rootstock on which varieties used in Europe are grafted, while it was *V. labrusca* that was more often used for making wine. *V. labrusca*, the main example of which is the Concord grape, makes a wine that gives off an almost rank aroma—or, as Jancis Robinson puts it in her *Vines, Grapes and Wines*, "oozing the musky smell of a wet and rather cheap fur coat which wine tasters have agreed to call 'foxy' in their tasting notes." Attempts have been made to cross it with other grapes, but in almost every case (Seyval Blanc is one exception), the foxy odor of *V. labrusca* dominated in the resulting wine. Nevertheless, at least it survived under American conditions and made wine production possible, although it must be said that, throughout the nineteenth century, reported reactions of those who had tasted French or German wine were that American-made wine was bad, even verging on the undrinkable. However, with American victory in the Mexican-American War of 1848–49, the Southwest and California were annexed by the United States—and California, where vines for winemaking were first planted by the Spanish Franciscan missionary Father Junipero Serra in 1769, brought V. *vinifera* into the Union. Subsequently, when discussing American wines, some commentators made an exception for wine from California. In defense of the major V. *labrusca* grape, the Concord, it is profitably used for grape juice and grape jelly on a commercial scale, and there has evolved a sweet wine that many enjoy.

What can you do with leftover wine?

BOTH AT HOME and in restaurants, it is often only two people who share a bottle of wine. Now that so much wine has such high levels of alcohol (over 14 percent alcohol is very common for reds), two people sharing a standard bottle (750 ml in volume) could feel unpleasantly inebriated, as well as feeling guilty at exceeding the daily alcohol consumption recommended by doctors. An up-market British supermarket chain has launched a range of 500 ml bottles so that their customers (the middle-class ones about whose drinking habits the British government is becoming concerned) are neither tempted to overindulge nor annoyed by the waste when they don't finish the bottle.

But if one does start with a standard 750 ml bottle and has wine left over, what should one do with it? The problem is that if you leave, say, 250 ml of wine in a 750 ml bottle, even if recorked or with the screw cap put back on, the oxygen in the air above the wine will still attack the alcohol quite rapidly and form acetic acid (the main constituent of vinegar after water) and ethyl acetate. The wine will not be terribly nice to drink.

The classic answer is to use the leftover wine for making a

sauce in cooking the next day. A red wine sauce for two boneless steaks might be made as follows. Put olive oil in the frying pan, cook chopped shallots in it till yellow, pour out the contents of the pan into a bowl through a metal strainer, put aside the strainer with the filtered-off shallot, and return the olive oil in the bowl to the pan. Now put in the steaks, which you have already seasoned on both sides with salt and pepper. Fry for five minutes on either side (for a one-inch steak). While you are doing this, boil the 250 ml of leftover red wine in a small pot until the alcohol has boiled off (as judged by passing a flame over the pot)—the particularly nasty ethyl acetate has a lower boiling point than alcohol and will have boiled off as well. Put the cooked steaks on plates preheated in a 200°F oven and gently pour away the olive oil. Add the still-hot wine to the pan and also the shallot from the strainer. Resume heating the pan and scrape off any meat residues from the pan with a wooden spoon. Reduce the volume and add butter according to taste. Take the plates with the steaks out of the oven and divide the red wine/shallot/butter sauce over them. Serve with vegetables and a freshly opened bottle of red wine.

But if the wine one has not consumed is really good, it would be a terrible waste not to keep it drinkable for the next day. The chemistry is simple in principle: it will go off more slowly the less "head space" there is above the wine; it will go bad more slowly the lower the temperature at which it is stored overnight; and it will go off more slowly if the head space is not air at normal pressure but a blanketing inert gas or a partial vacuum provided by the air-pumping-out devices one can buy in the shops. You will preserve your wine reasonably well if you keep around some third (250 ml), half (375 ml), and two-thirds (500 ml) bottles, put your undrunk wine in the appropriately sized bottle, pump out the head space, and keep the wine in the refrigerator overnight. You just need to remember to take it out of the refrigerator long enough before you drink it to get it up to the right temperature.

On the other hand, champagne and other sparkling wines keep very easily. Just put the bottle back in the refrigerator without bothering to stopper it. The slow evolution of carbon dioxide bubbles will keep the air away for a long time before the wine goes flat.

Ceremonial: should you turn your back on the loving cup?

SPARE A THOUGHT for King Edward the Martyr, slain in 978 at Corfe Castle in Dorset—some say by his own mother, Aelfryth—while raising his hands to drink. The drinking horns were heavy and took both hands to raise; the body was thus exposed and vulnerable to a knife blow.

And so (it is said) began the custom of the loving cup, still practiced by livery companies, the Inns of Court, many Oxford and Cambridge colleges, and similar institutions. Inexplicable unless you know a little of its underlying purpose, the loving-cup ceremonial becomes clear if you think of Edward.

The two-handled cup, usually of silver or silver gilt, is filled with wine or a spiced wine often referred to as "sack" (see p. 20 for a different interpretation) and passed around the tables. Each person on receiving the cup bows to the one who handed it to him, on the right, and to their neighbor on the left. The one on the right remains standing; the one on the left rises and holds the cup cover in his right, or dagger, hand. Thus while the drinker is taking his wine, he is protected on the right, and watching the potential assailant on his left, who in any case is disarmed by the cover.

It sounds more complex than it is, but although it may now seem otiose, like all ceremonial it exists in commemoration of something that once was real. And like all ceremonial, too, there are constant arguments about whether the protector should stand facing away from the drinker or, literally, watch his back.

We would probably take the latter position, since it's the one adopted by the Worshipful Company of Armourers and Brasiers, who should really know all about such things if anyone does.

Wine, women, and what was the other one?

THERE IS A venerable rhetorical figure called the *hendiatris*, consisting of three words joined together to express one idea. "Lock, stock and barrel" comes to mind, as do "sex, drugs and rock 'n' roll," "liberty, equality, and fraternity," and, indeed, "blood, sweat and tears."

But there can be few more appealing than "wine, women, and song." The three stand or fall together as an image of the good earthly life—at least, the good earthly life if you happen to like all three.

Wine and women? A house of ill fame, perhaps. Wine and song? A drunken knees-up. Women and song? A gospel choir. But all three together: ah, there's lovely, as they say in Wales.

But who first said it? The usual answer is also the strangest. The couplet is generally given in German, as in the epigraph of John Addington Symonds's book of medieval German student songs, published in 1884:

> *Wer liebt nicht Weib Wein und Gesang*
> *Der bleibt ein Narr sein Lebenslang.*

Literally, "Who loves not wine women and song / Remains a fool his whole life long."

And to whom does Symonds, without doubt or hesitation, attribute the couplet? Why, none other than Martin Luther, the great reformer and founder of the Lutheran Church.

It seems somehow improbable, and there are cracks around the attribution into which refreshing incredulity can creep. For a start, the phrase has equivalents in many languages and cultures: "*Sur, sura, sundari*" in Sanskrit; "*Piker, vin, og sang*" in Norwegian; in Polish "*Wino, kobiety, i spiew*"; in Swedish "*Vin, kvinnor, och sång*"; and in Czech, "*Víno, ûeny a zpev.*" It is hard to believe they all nicked the phrase from Luther, particularly the speakers of Sanskrit.

Yet Luther was no teetotaler, and the services of the church that bore his name produced some of the greatest and most joyful music of all time, including the masses of Michael Praetorius and the music of J. S. Bach. Nor was he a celibate; indeed, he condemned celibacy, and wrote to a friend:

I shall never take a wife, as I feel at present. Not that I am insensible to my flesh or sex (for I am neither wood nor stone); but my mind is averse to wedlock because I daily expect the death of a heretic.

The heretic was, of course, himself. And in due course, he wrote, "suddenly, and while I was occupied with far different thoughts the Lord has plunged me into marriage." He was forty-two and his new wife, Katharina—a former nun whom he had arranged to smuggle out of the convent in a herring barrel—was twenty-six; by all accounts, theirs was a thoroughly happy marriage.

So it *could* have been that Luther, knowing the triad already, merely turned it into a catchy verse. The great travel writer Patrick Leigh Fermor, in *A Time of Gifts* (which describes his walk from London to Constantinople in the 1930s), first enters Germany at a town called Goch, where, in an inn named At the Sign of the Black Eagle, he sees the verse painted "right across the walls" in "bold Gothic black-letter script." Yet he sees it again, in the second of his trilogy, *Between the Woods and the Water*, this time in Romania. He remarks on this to the landlord, saying he'd seen it before in Goch; the landlord

> laughed and asked me if I knew who the poet was. "No? It was Martin Luther." I was rather surprised. Unlike the Lutheran Saxons, the Swabians were all Catholics.

It's possible, then, that the attribution was some sort of slur against Luther. Possible, too, is that the rhyme was simply around, in the air, and Luther seemed a good person to attribute it to, just as it is as impossible to remove the quote "All that is necessary for evil to triumph is that the good do nothing" from its attribution to Edmund Burke as it is to find out where he said it.

The *Oxford Dictionary of Quotations* gives the attribution to Luther but acknowledges that there is "no proof of authorship." Its transatlantic rival, *Bartlett's Familiar Quotations*, offers the German poet Johann Heinrich Voss (1751–1826) as the most likely candidate. But in truth, it remains a mystery. Enough to say that we should all applaud the sentiment and raise a glass to the author—whoever he was.

What links wine and olives?

SOME DECADES AGO, an Oxford University history examination paper asked, "Liberty never flourishes where the orange tree grows. Discuss." The Mediterranean is where the orange, the olive, and the vine all flourish, and, at the time, Spain, Portugal, and Greece were all dictatorships. The Fascist dictatorship in Italy was a relatively recent memory. (Fortunately, the question seemed to ignore California and Florida.)

But to the visitor to these countries, there is a magical relationship between the citrus fruits, the deep green olive trees, the wine, Homer's "wine-dark sea," and the smell in the Greek forests of the resin that flavors the national wine, retsina. The longevity of Mediterranean peoples is often attributed to their consumption of olive oil, red wine, and fish. Olive oil, like wine, is obtained by the pressing of a fruit, and like wine it comes in many grades and at many prices. It differs in not being fermented. In earlier times, olive oil and wine, being easily kept over the winter, provided people with a source of calories when other sources were relatively scarce.

The Romans used to float olive oil on top of wine as a way of preserving it. The olive oil would have slowed down the rate at which oxygen in the air attacked the wine. Indeed, the olive oil is evident in the oldest (fourth-century) glass wine bottle to have survived, now on display in Speyer, Germany. After a domestic experiment, we are pleased to confirm that it works.

How did wine affect American civil rights across 2,250 years?

WINE CAN HAVE a long reach—in this case, well over two thousand years. In 1917, the case of *Buchanan v. Warley* reached the U.S. Supreme Court, which ruled unanimously that a Louisville, Kentucky, ordinance demanding racial segregation was unconstitutional. Specifically, it was in breach of the Fourteenth Amendment, which required states to provide equal protection to all people—not just citizens—under their jurisdiction; in this case, the issue was the protection of the right to own and to dispose of property. It was one of the many landmark cases in the last century's dismantling of embedded racism, and the first to declare that this kind of ordinance was in breach of the constitution.

Commentators on the case have recalled the words of Judge David Brewer. Writing in 1893, twenty-five years after the Fourteenth Amendment was ratified, Brewer argued that constitutions

represent the deliberate judgment of the people as to the provisions and restraints which, firmly and fully enforced, will secure to each citizen the greatest liberty and utmost protection. They are rules proscribed [*sic*] by Philip sober to control Philip drunk.

But who was Philip, and why drunk, and why sober?

The Philip in question was King Philip II of Macedon, the father of Alexander the Great. Philip, who reigned from 356 to 336 BC, was the final judge of appeal in Macedonia. He also acquired a fine military education while held hostage in Thebes as a child, and whether he learned it there or of his own accord, he was notoriously fond of wine. The story goes that one old woman appealed to him against a court judgment. Slurring somewhat, he rejected her appeal, at which point she shouted, "I appeal."

The king, slightly bemused, inquired precisely whom she was appealing to.

"I appeal," she replied, "from Philip drunk to Philip sober."

The king agreed to reconsider her appeal at a later date, and her words passed into history.

But not everywhere. It is, for example, technically impossible for a British member of Parliament to be drunk in the debating chamber since 1945, when the cry of "Not sober!" was banned. Not that it affected Alan Clark, the notable wine bibber and serial adulterer who was told off by Clare Short, MP, for speaking in the chamber "in this condition." Clark's diaries reveal precisely what condition he was in and how he got there: "A Palmer '61, then a '75 for comparison, before switching back to '61, a delicious Pichon Longueville."

Philip drunk would have approved. Philip sober, however . . .

Should wine be decanted?

IS DECANTING WINE a necessity, a ritual, or one-upmanship? Are you decanting to improve or to impress? Some wines, especially vintage port, have a lot of deposit. Serving guests directly from the bottle is unsatisfactory, because the wine inevitably gets agitated as it is taken around the table, with the result that the guests get altogether too much deposit in their glasses. The traditional solution to the problem is decanting. First of all, the bottle is stood up for some hours—ideally, at least twenty-four—to enable the sediment to drop gently to the bottom of the bottle; then a steady hand pours the wine gently but in a single go into another vessel (a fine antique decanter or a simple jug function equally well). A light beneath the neck—traditionally a candle—shows when the deposit is about to pass over from the bottle, and the decanting is stopped. (This raises the question of what to do with what is left in the bottle. Passing it through a filter paper such as is used for coffee making seems to be fine, although it is preferable to use the unbleached brown-colored ones.)

So far, so uncontentious. The controversial question is whether decanting benefits those wines that lack a significant deposit. Decanting wine aerates it in the pouring and then leaves a large surface area of it exposed to the air. The longer the wine is subsequently left in the decanter before drinking, the more it will be exposed to the oxygen in the air—but will this be for good or ill? It is indisputable that the oxygen in the air attacks the alcohol in the wine from the moment the bottle is opened—this is why one pumps the air out of partly consumed bottles of wine so as to try to preserve them for pleasurable drinking the following day. Therefore, argued the renowned professor Émile Peynaud of the Institut d'Oenologie at the University of Bordeaux, the aeration of a sound wine through decanting is indefensible. (He acknowledged that some faulty, nasty-tasting wines might improve with aeration.) The majority in the Bordeaux wine trade do not agree with their late local expert—decanting of wine before drinking is generally favored, even for up to four hours. Hugh Johnson recommends aeration of almost all red wines and the majority of whites. David Bird, though like Peynaud a scientist, sides with Johnson, at least for younger wines.

A recent blind tasting comparing decanted and undecanted fine Bordeaux wines did not resolve the dispute. It suggested that while some are improved by seventy-five minutes in the decanter, others are made worse, but that only trial and error could determine which way a particular wine inclined. This scarcely amounts to useful guidance: after decanting, it's too late.

But why would anyone want a swizzle stick?

THE TERM *swizzle stick* is generally used now to refer to a little plastic paddle used to stir your take-out coffee. But go to an antiques dealer and that is not what you'll be offered. Instead, if they have any, you will be presented with an odd little cylinder, of silver or gold, out of which you can propel something that looks like a tiny cocktail umbrella without a covering. Half a dozen silver (or gold) wires will spring free like umbrella ribs, and there you go.

But where do you go? And why? And why "swizzle"?

The commonest explanation is that the swizzle stick is to stir the bubbles out of your champagne, which raises the question of why anyone would want to pay extra for wine with bubbles *in* it, only to pay even more extra for a device to get the bubbles *out*. This is one of those unanswerable questions of social history, but we can hazard a guess. The flibbertigibbet who takes a sip of champagne, sneezes, giggles, and says, "Oooh, the bubbles get up my nose!" is a legendary figure still with us, as you can see at any wedding. But there was a time—in the 1930s, the heyday of the swizzle stick—when giggling, sneezing, or performing any of the involuntary pneumatics associated with carbonated drinks was simply incompatible with the elegance and poise required of a woman. So (we humbly suggest) the swizzle stick in its retractable form was born, as a preemptive strike against the destabilizing bubble.

But why "swizzle"? The most likely answer there is that the word has been used for punches since the eighteenth century. We might reflect on whether the Englishman's classical education in the behavior of the ancient Greeks at their symposia (see p. 58) may have predisposed him to the idea of diluting his wine; we will never know. We do know that the earlier word *punch*, first seen in the early seventeenth century, comes from the Hindi *panch*, "five," referring to the five basic ingredients: wine (or brandy), water, lemon juice, sugar, and spice. And we know from personal experience that a glass of punch or swizzle needs the occasional stir, and stirring it with a spoon is likely to lead to spills and splashes; hence the traditional glass (or metal) rod, with a rounded end, is often used instead. And there we have it: a stick to stir your swizzle.

What would go nicely with curry?

PAIRING WINE and food used to be reasonably simple: the local wine and the local food would generally sit in harmony. Retsina with your *kokoretsi*, burgundy with *boeuf bourguignon*, a prosecco with *fegato alla veneziana*, a Bandol rosé with your bouillabaisse.

But globalization has made the task that much harder. We were rung up not so long ago by a friend who is best described not as an oenophile nor as a gourmet but by that seldom-heard word now, a *trencherman*. His work in the shipping industry takes him round the world, but he wanted to speak of a restaurant called, if he remembered correctly, Alberto, Feinstein, and Ho, which was, as far as he could recall, in Halifax, Nova Scotia. Alberto was Italian, Feinstein was originally from Vienna, and Ho was, as far as he knew, Vietnamese, and their cuisine, as well as their business venture, could be described by that portmanteau word for a multitude of gastronomic peculiarities, *fusion*.

Fusion, in this case, consisted of sweet-and-sour Wiener schnitzel with risotto, and when he asked what wine they recommended with the dish, the waiter replied, "Beer. Molson. Lots."

Indeed, the task would have been difficult to perform otherwise. A BBC radio producer was celebrated for his ability to construct satirical menus for special occasions, his chef d'oeuvre possibly being "vibrating skate wings lightly dusted with Ajax and served in a helmet," but reality has overtaken him: what would *you* choose to accompany a dish of udders cooked in hay, which we ate at one of the most celebrated restaurants in Britain?

But of all the challenges of food-and-wine pairings, the most insurmountable must surely be curry. Given that both the generic *balti* and chicken tikka masala have acquired the status of Britain's national dishes, the marketing of wines to accompany curry has become a fierce and valuable contest. Curry traditionally has been drunk with beer ever since the British Raj in the nineteenth century, when so-called India pale ales were brewed specifically to endure the four-thousand-mile voyage to India (you will still see IPA as a category on beer-pump handles in the pub).

The problem is compounded by the lack of any tradition of drinking with food in Indian culture: drinking, at least of alcohol, stops when eating starts, and food is usually accompanied by *lassi*, a sweet or salty drink made from yogurt—far better at taking the edge off a very hot curry, since only fat (as in yogurt) or sugar is effective at blunting the fire of the capsaicin in chiles.

One enterprising company, Balti Wine, was set up in 2007 specifically to crack this potential treasure chest with five wines, which they offer in various bottle-top colors to go with varying spiciness of food, "the product of extensive taste testing in conjunction with representatives from the Food Technology Department at Manchester University." Blended from Argentinian wines, they include Blue Top Sauvignon-Chardonnay for Mild Cuisine, Orange Top Chenin-Chardonnay for Medium Hot Cuisine, and Green Top Ugni Blanc–Chardonnay for the Hottest Cuisine, the last being described by wine writer Andrew Fraser as "quite unpleasant to drink on its own" but "transformed" with a lamb Karachi curry. Fraser ruefully concludes: "I certainly wish I'd thought of the idea."

Does the glass you use make any difference?

THIS IS A MATTER of some contention. There are several glassmakers who produce a series of glasses with different shapes for each type of wine; they insist that it makes a substantial difference in your tasting experience if you use a glass of a specific shape for claret, burgundy, chardonnay, riesling, or a dozen others. Many question this notion, saying that it is more of a marketing ploy than an absolute truth. There have been tastings in which glasses were marked against each other, but the results do not reliably point one way or another. In the circumstances, one might as well be guided by aesthetics and cost as by function.

Professionals at least can agree on the decision of the International Standards Organisation (ISO) to prescribe a standard tasting glass. This is used by tasters in wine competitions and also by examining bodies in wine-tasting examinations. The glass has a volume of 210 ml, but for tasting, only 50 ml of wine is put into it. The glass curves inward above the level to which it is thus filled, so as to capture 160 ml of aromas. There is also plenty of room for swirling. Fifty ml is adequate for tasting, but not in most cases for drinking, for which rather larger glasses should ideally be used. Even so, the same principle should be followed: the glass should be considerably less than half full so as to leave plenty of space for the aromas and for swirling, and it should curve inward from the level to which it is filled.

Clear glass is important for the appreciation of wine, because it allows the color to be observed, both at the "core" and at the rim, where surface tension provides a very thin layer rising up the inside of the glass (the meniscus). The color of the rim should be keenly observed. Generally, one can see the aging of red wine at the rim, which is purple for young wines, garnet to brick for mature ones, and brown for those of great age or distinctly past their peak. Therefore, colored wine glasses are not good for wine appreciation. Silver goblets, although not colored, are opaque and therefore are not ideal either.

Silver, nevertheless, is used for wine. It does not impart any noticeable taint to wine—hence its use in the necks of carafes and in funnels for wine. Historically, wine was often drunk or tasted from shallow silver dishes with one or two handles. They had the obvious advantage over glass vessels in that they could be carried around without risk of breakage, and were shallow enough to allow the color of red wine to be assessed. They would not have been very good for trapping aromas, however. In Scotland, dishes with two handles were known as quaiches (and were used for whisky and brandy as well as for wine); they are still manufactured

and given as christening gifts. The French equivalent is the one-handled tastevin, used exclusively for tasting, as the name implies. Antique tastevins can still be found; some have an ancient silver coin providing the base. The tastevin gave its name to a society set up in France in 1934 to promote the drinking of burgundy through unashamed ritual, the Confrèrerie des Chevaliers du Tastevin, which flourishes to this day.

China tea, yes—but Chinese wine?

CHINESE WINES do not exactly crowd the shelves of Western wine shops, so it may come as something of a surprise to learn that, as of 2007, China had the world's fifth largest vineyard area (although only one-sixth of the total grape harvest was used for wine) and produced nearly 5 percent of the world's output of wine. Furthermore, the making of wine has a long, if somewhat episodic, history in China. The great poet Li Bai, who lived from 701 to 762, wrote dozens of poems about wine, including "Song of the River":

> My boat is of ebony
> the holes in my flute are golden.
> As a plant takes out stains from silk
> so wine takes sadness from the heart.
> When one has good wine,
> a graceful boat,
> and a maiden's love,
> why envy the immortal gods?

This is not far from Omar Khayyám's celebration of a book of verses, a jug of wine, a loaf of bread, and thou, with Li Bai substituting flute music for verses. There is a certain rightness about the similarity, because China owed its acquisition of *Vitis vinifera*, the supreme species of wine-grape vine, to Persia.

Alcoholic beverages, including wine made from native grapes, had long been known in China, but it was only in 128 BC that the first seeds of *Vitis vinifera* arrived in the country. General Chang Chien was sent on an expedition to Bactria, and on his return to the Chinese court, he presented vine seeds to Emperor Han Wu Dia (Han Dynasty). They came from Fergana, the country east of Samarkand, which is now Uzbekistan but was then part of Persia. (In fact, the Chinese—and Japanese—word for grape is *budo*, while the late Persian word was *buda*.) The emperor had vines planted around the imperial palaces in Xinjiang and Shanxi, and three centuries later wine was so valuable that it was used as a diplomatic tool—perhaps much as the Austrian emperors were later to use Tokaji. Over the succeeding centuries, the planting of vines became more widespread and—depending on the level of tax—wine made from grapes, as opposed to that made from cereals, increased in popularity among the lower social classes.

Genghis Khan's grandson, Kublai Khan, who lived from 1216 to 1294, completed the conquest of China begun by his grandfather and founded the Yüan Dynasty. During his rule, the court chose grape wine (*putao jiu*) for the ceremony when worshiping their ancestors, while in 1291, a wine cellar was built in one of the imperial palaces. Marco Polo, in his description of his travels in the thirteenth century, wrote that "in Shanxi province grew many excellent vines, supplying a great deal of wine, and in all Cathay this is the only place where wine is produced. It is carried hence all over the country." For reasons nobody really knows, wine fell from favor during the Ming Dynasty (1368–1644). One possible explanation was that the first Ming emperor was born in the south of China, where the weather is not conducive to the growing of grapes, and thus lacked the wine culture present in the north. As well, the duty on grape wine was raised, making it less affordable for the less wealthy.

With the coming of the Ching (or Qing) Dynasty in 1644, the popularity of wine gradually recovered, doubtless helped by the enduring belief that it had health-giving properties. Emperor K'an-hi, who ruled at the same time as Louis XIV, experimented by planting vines in different parts of the country, which confirmed that they flourished in the north but not in the subtropical south. With the nineteenth century's influx of missionaries and invaders, however, foreign influence on the growing of grapes and the making of wine grew. In the mid-nineteenth century,

Jesuit missionaries encouraged the planting of vineyards specifically to make wine for use during the celebration of the sacraments. In the late nineteenth century, French Catholic missionaries planted vineyards and made wine. During the German and Japanese occupations from the late nineteenth and into the early twentieth centuries, a winery was established by the Germans and another by the Japanese. Most important, however, was the establishing of the first modern Chinese winery. Chang Bi Shi, referred to variously as an overseas Chinese merchant or as an officer in the Qing government, returned to China in 1892 and set up the Chang Yu winery in Yantai, reportedly employing the Austrian consul as winemaker. He also introduced 150 varieties of V. *vinifera* from Europe, including Welschriesling, which remains of importance for the wine industry today.

It might have been thought that wine would have been a victim of the Communist victory in 1949, but this was not the case. Indeed, the government expanded the wineries: they preferred that the people drink wine rather than spirits, and they and successive governments wanted to reserve rice for food rather than allow it to be used to make rice wine. However, for reasons of economy, the grape wine was blended with water, other fruit juices, coloring, and fermented cereals, as a result of which people became confused as to what wine really was. Nowadays, it is necessary to specify grape wine.

After 1979, foreign investors were allowed to establish a modern wine industry. Substantial investment was made by a number of Western distilleries, who imported vinification equipment, V. *vinifera* vine cuttings, and the technical expertise needed to make the wines, and Western-style wines were produced. In the 1990s, a wine boom was sparked off when officials followed the lead of Western countries in recommending the moderate use of red wine to reduce the risk of heart disease. As a result, thousands of cases were imported and rushed onto the market, tankers of bulk wine arrived to be bottled locally, and small wineries sprang up all over China. By the mid-2000s, a number of large château-style wineries had been established.

Wine, especially champagne, is now wildly fashionable, but at the summit are the Bordeaux *grands crus*, including the most expensive wines of the Right Bank. When the élites first came into contact with red wines, most found them too bitter to drink with pleasure. However, status demanded that first-growth Bordeaux be drunk, so Sprite would be added to soften and round out the wine. Horror stories abounded of customers mixing Château Pétrus and Coke. True connoisseurs have now emerged, but so have collectors, with the result that they are among those most responsible for driving up the prices of the first growths, which now are bought but seldom drunk. With continuing economic growth and growing awareness of wine, however, a true wine-drinking culture will almost certainly develop, which should encourage the export to China of wines from all over the world. By then, the addition of Coke will undoubtedly no longer be necessary.

Do they really make wine from bees?

THIS IS A question that, while it has not exactly haunted us since someone first mentioned "bee wine," occasionally and without warning springs worryingly to mind. After all, there's hardly a vegetable on the planet that hasn't been made into wine, so . . . can you ferment an animal? If so, we can be sure that someone has done it.

But books are not only a (hopefully) diverting way for the reader to while away an hour or two; they also give pleasure to the authors, giving them an excuse to look into things that otherwise might have gone unresolved.

We confess our initial thought was that yes, there probably was bee wine, and yes, it probably was made from bees in some way; if not, it likely was an epithet for mead.

We were mostly wrong. Yes, there is bee wine, but it has nothing to do with bees and everything to do with the yeast, which is introduced into the must in the form of a yeast-and-sugar lump that rises and falls with the fermentation process, bumping around like a bee in a bottle.

On balance, we're relieved. On balance too, though, we wish we hadn't found out about the animal wines of Indochina: Seahorse wine, water-snake wine, King Cobra wine, Many Snakes wine, and, indeed, Bamboo Bee Wine. Each bottle has the animal inside it. Of course, it's not actually *wine* wine, and the Bamboo Bee isn't actually a *bee* bee, but all the same . . . all the same . . .

Is there wine in Paradise?

IT'S A GOOD question, and one that has received little attention from the wine-drinking believers in an afterlife, who just sort of *assume* that Paradise will be like life on earth, only better. Of *course* there'll be wine in Paradise. How could it possibly be otherwise?

But for the abstemious faiths, it is a problem. Muslims, in particular, have been exercised over the centuries by non-Muslims saying things like "Oh, go on, just have one glass—after all, there'll be wine in Paradise."

Commentators on the Qur'an have come up with answers to such silliness, of course, and our favorite refers to Hadith 589, narrated by Abu Huraira:

> The Prophet said, "Allah said, 'I have prepared for My righteous slaves (such excellent things) as no eye has ever seen, nor an ear has ever heard nor a human heart can ever think of.'"

So as we can see paradise is something that is not of this world. So when the Qur'an talks about rivers of honey that does not mean that it is the same kind of honey that we have in this world. Similarly, when the Qur'an talks about rivers of wine in paradise that does not mean that it is the same kind of wine that we have here on earth that makes you get drunk and do stupid things and gives you a hangover the next morning. No, not at all. God is just using these terms in order for us to try to imagine what this paradise is kind of like. So the wine of paradise is nothing like the wine of this world.

Theology is a wonderful thing. Perhaps the wine of Paradise, which is not like the wine of this world, bears some relation to the drunkenness of Purim (see p. 26), which is not like the drunkenness of this world. Such speculations are outside our qualifications. All we can do is hope that it all turns out for the best . . .

When is wine not wine?

THE FIGURE OF speech that dominates this book is the *erotema*, the official word for what we usually call a "rhetorical question."

We give you this bit of information as a sort of consolation prize because—unlike all the other questions, which we go on to answer—we really don't know the answer to this one.

The scene is an agreeable house in the Vaucluse region of Provence, within a stone's throw (and sometimes we wish we had done) of Peter Mayle, author of *A Year in Provence*. The house has some land attached. On that land are vines. The vines are cultivated by a local farmer who, by way of rent, hands back a certain amount of the wine he makes from them.

It is late summer, shading into early autumn. We arrive back from the nearby village to find a case of bottles in the porch. They are unlabeled but clearly contain white wine. We prepare a modest lunch and open a bottle: what fun! The *vin* doesn't come more *du pays* than this.

We share a bottle with our companion: it is unsophisticated, slightly sweet, but otherwise nothing to complain about. But we notice at the end of lunch that there is none of that gentle elevation you'd expect, none of that feeling that it's siesta time and not a moment too soon. Maybe (we think) it is simply weak. We open another bottle. We drink it. We look at each other.

"Anything?"

"No. You?"

"Nope. Stone cold sober."

Hmm. We wonder whether we are somehow fooling ourselves and this is grape juice. We decide on an experiment. We pour a glass into a small pan and heat it to a little below boiling point, then light a match and hold it over the pan. There is a gentle *paf* and a blue flame ignites.

Grape juice does not give off anything that, when heated, bursts into flame.

We repeat the experiments—both the drinking experiment and the flame experiment—several times over the next few days, with identical results. At the end of the process we have three pieces of information:

1. The stuff is made from grapes; of that there is no doubt.
2. When heated, it gives off a volatile and inflammable hydrocarbon.
3. That hydrocarbon is not alcohol.

Perhaps this is some new experiment in winemaking. If so, it seems unlikely to catch on. If any reader can explain precisely what this agreeable but perplexing beverage actually *was*, they might be good enough to write in to the publisher and let us know. The prize will be a bottle of the fabled wine of Antipaxos (see p. 117).

Who wrote an elegy to a wineglass?

THERE IS SOMETHING about the sight of an empty glass that can move the soul to poetry. Sometimes the more sensitive of the company can be moved to recite the closing ruba'i of Omar Khayyám (see p. 17):

> And when like her, oh Saki, you shall pass
> Among the Guests star-scatter'd on the Grass,
> And in your joyous errand reach the spot
> Where I made one—turn down an empty Glass!

How does one top that? As always, we have the answer. A simple reference to a poem addressed simultaneously to a wineglass and extolling German wine should do the trick, and we have just the thing: "Auf das Trinkglas," by Justinus Kerner, a doctor, city medical officer, and author of a treatise on animal magnetism.

Here it is, in all its glory: *to the drinking glass of a dead friend.*

> O wondrous glass, you empty lie,
> Which he would raise with joyful hand;
> The spider now around you spins
> A web of somber mourning-band.

> But now you fill for me anew
> Moon-bright with gold of German vines
> And in your deep and holy glow
> I cast my solemn trembling gaze.

> What in your depths I may discern
> Is not for every human heart

But in that moment, I well know
That friend from friend can never part.

And in this truth, my dearest glass,
I raise, and drain you joyfully!
And see the mirror'd golden stars
Clear-cupp'd in your most precious blood.

The silent moon moves o'er the vale,
The solemn midnight bell doth toll.
The glass is drained! The holy note
Sounds yet within thy crystal bowl.

It is, of course, somewhat better in the original German. But it's certainly worth its weight in one-upmanship, and if you encounter any resistance, you can add that it was set to music by Schumann (*Kerner-Liederreihe*, Op. 35, No. 8). What was the "gold of German vines" that the dead friend "often raised with joy"? Oh, probably a riesling, we'd say; wouldn't you agree?

What was the Judgment of Paris?

THERE WERE, of course, more than one, so the answer depends on which one you mean. The first judgment reportedly took place more than three thousand years ago on Mount Ida, overlooking the Troäd, the region in northwest Asia Minor whose capital was the city of Troy. Eris, the Goddess of Discord, had not been invited to the wedding of Peleus and Thetis (later the parents of Achilles). In anger, she threw a golden apple labeled "To the Fairest" into the midst of the guests at the wedding feast. The guests included the twelve immortal gods and goddesses of Olympus, and three of the goddesses claimed it: Hera, queen of the heavens, wife of Zeus, and inferior only to him in power; Athena, goddess of war and wisdom; and Aphrodite, goddess of love and beauty. Zeus wisely refused to adjudicate among them, advising them to seek out Paris (then disguised as a herdsman on Mount Ida, but in reality a son of Priam, the king of Troy) and present their claims. The three goddesses appeared before Paris, told him what they wished him to do, and agreed to accept his decision. Hera promised to make him the ruler of all Asia; Athena promised him victory in all battles, as well as wisdom and beauty; and Aphrodite promised him the fairest woman in the world as his wife. Paris awarded the golden apple, the Apple of Discord, to Aphrodite, and thereby won the eternal hatred of Hera and Athena for himself and for all Trojans. Aphrodite's promise was kept: Paris did acquire the fairest woman in the world, Helen, the wife of Menelaus, king of Sparta, but only by stealing her and taking her with him back to Troy. The war against Troy was fought to recover Helen, possessor, according to Christopher Marlowe, of "the face which launched a thousand ships and burnt the topless towers of Ilium." With the two outraged goddesses, Hera and Athena, on the side of the Greeks, the destruction of Troy and the extinction of its royal family were tragically ensured.

The second Judgment of Paris was rather less earthshaking—except perhaps to those closely involved. A young Englishman, Steven Spurrier, owned a wine shop in Paris called Caves de la Madeleine; in addition, he and an American colleague, Patricia Gallagher, together ran a wine school, l'Académie du Vin. As a way of making the school better known, they set up a competition between French and California wines. They wanted to bring the rapidly improving California wines to the notice of the Europeans, but Spurrier confidently expected the French wines to win. The year was 1976, the bicentennial of the American Declaration of Independence, used by Spurrier as the publicity handle to bring the competition to public notice.

It was decided that the competition would concentrate on white burgundies versus California chardonnays and on French Bordeaux wines versus California cabernet sauvignons. Of the eleven judges, nine were French, with Spurrier and Gallagher the other two. The wines were tasted blind. To the anger, astonishment, and chagrin of the French judges, a 1973 California chardonnay from Chateau Montelena and a 1973 California cabernet sauvignon from Stag's Leap Wine Cellars, both from the Napa Valley, were ranked first in the competition (the second places were taken by, respectively, Meursault Charmes Roulot 1973 and Château Mouton-Rothschild 1970). At least one of the French judges demanded the return of her scorecards—Spurrier refused—while another explained the red wine rankings by arguing that American wines matured more quickly than did their French counterparts and therefore the latter would not show as well that early in their cycle, thus rendering the whole exercise null and void. The French and California wine worlds were shaken. The Greeks of the ancient world had considered the destruction of Troy, with its attendant slaughter and desecration of sacred places, as signifying the end of the Age of Heroes; this had been caused by the Judgment of Paris. There were those who saw the outcome of the second Judgment of Paris as the equivalent destruction of the overworshipped reputations of the heroes of Bordeaux.

In 2006 Spurrier again thought that it would be amusing to have a Franco-California competition, during which exactly the same red wines, now aged by a further thirty years, would be matched against one another. This time there were two juries, one sitting in California and one sitting in London; their marks were combined to produce the eventual winners. A California wine again came first: this was the Ridge Montebello 1971, which had come fifth in 1976; the second place went to Stag's Leap Wine Cellars 1973, the winner in 1976. It was decided that the white burgundies versus chardonnays tasting, however, should not try to replicate the earlier contestants, as the wines could not be expected to show well after thirty years. It was also decided to look at a recent vintage for the reds, so five Bordeaux wines from 2000 and one from 2001 were tasted against six California cabernet sauvignons from, variously, the 2000, 2001, and 2002 vintages. The result for the white wines was that a French wine, Puligny-Montrachet Les Purcelles 2002 Domaine Leflaive, came first; the next four were California chardonnays, with the wine from Chateau Montelena, whose 1973 had won in 1976, coming seventh. As for the younger vintages, Château Margaux 2000 came first by a considerable margin, with the next four places filled by California wines; the wine from Ridge came third, while that from Stag's Leap Wine Cellars came fifth.

There was satisfaction in measure for both sides in this second tasting. On the one hand, the results demonstrated that outstanding California wines could age well, a notion about which the French were extremely skeptical in 1976 (and the Americans a bit fearful). On the other hand, in 2006, younger French wines came in top in both the competition between burgundies and California chardonnays and that between younger Bordeaux and California cabernet sauvignons. Honor was saved.

Whatever happened to the Nicolas vans?

TALKING OF PARIS . . . Things come, and things go. Mostly we don't notice, but a recent Internet forum raised the question: What was around when you were twenty-one years old that has completely vanished now?

Our first thought was: Paris.

Nonsense, of course. Paris is still there. But it is not the same Paris; in a few short years, the city has entirely changed. Now it is a modern European capital, in many ways indistinguishable from any other modern European capital. But back in the 1970s it was palpably different. It smelled different, it looked different; it even sounded different. The majestic peculiarity of its Citroën cars, so idiosyncratic that even their hydraulic fluid was different, made from vegetables. The *zinc* in every café on every corner. The hats the policemen wore. The idea of starting the day with a pousse-café. The ability, unthinkable to an Englishman, to get a drink *whenever you wanted one*. The cheapness and ubiquity of perfectly drinkable wine. The pervasive and evocative smell of black caporal tobacco. The list is endless.

But the first thing that occurred to us about the Paris that has gone is: whatever happened to the Nicolas vans? They were like British milk trucks, and every morning they would hum and rattle along the streets delivering the unpretentious but marginally drinkable Nicolas table wines, not to restaurants and wine merchants and bars, but to people's private houses. The wine truck would draw up, the wine man would hop out, a couple of bottles would be deposited on the step or handed to the householder or *concièrge*, and off he would glide again, to stop again a few doors down.

It was, perhaps above anything else, the great signifier of French exceptionalism and *savoir-vivre*. In Britain, what you got delivered to your home by a man in an electric vehicle each morning was milk, which was healthy and pure and good for you. In France? Wine. Wine that they would drink with their dinner whether there was company or not and even if nobody had died or had a baby. Wine that was so much part of life that it arrived automatically, like a staple.

Now we see that the Parisians were right, and wine is indeed a staple: a staple, in correct moderation, of good living, of good fellowship, of the daily pleasures of the table and the home.

But what have they decided among themselves? Have they changed their minds? *Whatever has happened to the Nicolas vans?*

Why did the sommelier weep?

THERE ARE TIMES in every life, no matter how well regulated, when we might wish that we were paid to do what we love. For the wine drinker, the glitter of a sommelier's tastevin—a mere spoon to the outside world, a hard-won badge of honor as noble as an episcopal miter to the wearer—is enough to set off a fantasy of spending one's life moving, with a certain affable dignity, among pleasant and appreciative diners, recommending a wine here, commending a choice there, guiding the novice and exchanging a few words of mutual respect with the connoisseur.

But the sommelier's life is not always an easy one. Indeed, the sommelier himself is less frequently seen than previously, as dining out becomes less of a truly special occasion, and as restaurants themselves slug it out in increasingly competitive markets.

Yet there was a time when any eating house that thought itself more than a mere chop house or bistro would have its sommelier, and none more so than those once bleakly grand, now slightly faded, "Business and Commercial Hotels" that stood, immovable as an alderman's watch chain, in every large British city.

It was in one such hotel that we dined alone one evening. The dining room, which magically smelled as British hotel dining rooms were meant to smell—of gravy, soup, damp, and the poetry of Philip Larkin—was half full; all except one of the occupied tables was taken by a pair of men doing business. It was sad to see these probably harmless chaps spending an evening in the Midlands rain telling lies to each other ("We're very confident in the prospects statesidewise"), while the one couple, a man and a woman obviously married and equally obviously not to each other, attracted such glances of loathing and envy that we half expected to see them run shrieking from the room.

There was, of course, a sommelier: a worn-down, rotund, small man with a hairdo reminiscent of Dirk Bogarde's in the last reel of *Death in Venice*. He moved sadly from table to table like a miniaturized Alfred Hitchcock, gloomily dispensing wine from the lower end of the list to people who swilled it around the glass, swigged at it, and declared whether or not they liked it. This was, of course, lèse-majesté of the first order: according to the old school, the sommelier's job is to protect his customers from a dud bottle of wine, whether because they are about to make a poor choice or because something is wrong with the bottle they've been brought.

But this sommelier had been ground down over the years until he projected himself not as an expert guide, but as a mere delivery system.

Sad and alone in this forlorn morgue, we ordered a bottle of a rather good St. Julien to elevate, however artificially and transiently, the mood. It came. The sommelier drew the cork. His tastevin, we noticed, was tarnished. He poured a little into the glass and waited. We raised the glass to the nose, swirled lightly, and inhaled.

His hand began to move the bottle toward the glass.

"Actually," we murmured, "perhaps . . . is this bottle corked?"

His hand trembling slightly, he raised the tastevin on its chain, poured in a few drops, and inhaled. He picked up the cork and smelled that.

"It is," he said. "Yes. It is."

He seemed disconsolate and stood there for a moment, silent, what looked like the beginning of tears in his eyes. Had we offended him mortally? Was this the wine on which, to the harsh, money-grasping management, he had staked his reputation? *Why was he so sad?*

"Do you know, sir," he said, sniffing, "I have been working here for twenty-eight years and I can't remember when a customer last rejected a bottle on the grounds that it was corked, when it actually *was* corked." He became confidential. "Most of them," he said, "you could give them yesterday's leavings, mixed up and resealed, and they'd say, 'Mmm, yes, delicious, they do me very well here, you know.' And the ones that do complain, they're complaining because they don't like it or it's not what they thought it would be. But a corked bottle which really *is* . . . honestly, it's a treat. It's like the old days. Corked," he said, perking up. "*Corked.* Well, well. I'll bring you another, straightaway."

And off he glided, as if on air.

We all dream of being paid for what we enjoy. But as they say, be careful what you wish for, lest you get it.

Do you understand winespeak?

REGULAR BUYERS of wine probably read wine columnists and wine guides. They may wonder which guides to trust: what do the adjectives and nouns really mean? These are important questions. The conscientious writer tries to convey the experience you will have if you drink the wine, and this requires some detail. What most people probably want to know is, what does the wine taste like, and will they like it? Flavor, however, is actually made up of two components: its "nose" and its taste. The skeptic about the importance of its aroma should try drinking a glass while holding his or her nose. Certainly, part of the fun of drinking wine is catching the differences between what a wine smells like and what it tastes like. For many, the nose is almost more interesting, because layers of smell are sometimes more complex and easier to discern than layers of taste.

Indeed, the aroma (of a youngish wine) or bouquet (of a more mature wine) has produced some arresting characterizations of individual types of wine. One, ascribed to the writer Jancis Robinson, a Master of Wine, is for wine made from the Sauvignon Blanc grape, whether a Sancerre from the Loire or the eponymous wine from New Zealand: "cat's pee on a gooseberry bush." Now, let us think about that. The scent of gooseberries, yes, nettles, and sometimes elderflowers, and often grass and some herbs, but the cat's pee is more difficult. What if you do not own a cat? Would you recognize this particular scent? Even more to the point, would this description encourage you to buy it? Another columnist's recent description of a certain New Zealand sauvignon blanc was that it reminded him of "a rugby club changing room": we can only hope that this was more dismissive than descriptive. Another characterization, ascribed to a notable writer on burgundy, is that "great burgundy smells like shit." Again, let us think about it. The classic fruit scent for wine made from the Pinot Noir grape in Burgundy is raspberries, while for some of us, the faint scent of rubber is a possible clue. But his arresting descriptor? Does he mean the faint composty bouquet that can accompany fine wines? Or does he actually mean that arising from the less salubrious section of a farmyard? In any case, it is difficult to see the comment pinned on the shelf of your favorite wine shop. Or what about the classic Australian description of mature shiraz (syrah) as having a "sweaty saddle character"?

Wine columnists often pile on the more agreeable nouns. Here is one that described a Chilean wine made from the Cabernet Sauvignon grape: "gobs of fruit, blackcurrants and dark berries, notes of leather and pencil shavings, a hint of licorice, chocolate, and coffee." There can be several responses to that. You could pour a glass of the wine, sniff it, swirl it and sniff it again, and try, with increasing desperation, to find each of these scents. You could consider whether you really wanted to buy and drink a wine that smelled of pencil shavings. You could give up on the smells and taste it, trying to tease out everything promised by the adjectives. Or you could quote Jancis Robinson's reported comment that few can really discern more than a small handful of scents and tastes and just pour yourself a glass, drink it, and decide whether or not you like it.

What appears to lure consumers into the shops are the adjectives describing fruit—whether it is tropical fruit and melons for Australian chardonnay, blackcurrants for claret from the Médoc and especially from cabernet sauvignons from the New World, or dark cherries from an Italian Valpolicella—as well as vanilla from heavily oaked wines. What often happens is that the scents on the nose seldom translate directly into tastes in the mouth. Some do, of course, particularly the aggressively fruity New World wines. However, perhaps we should be thankful that leather, pencil shavings, rubber, stone, and compost seldom do. One of the more interesting disjunctures can happen with dry Alsace or German rieslings of some age, when the honey on the nose does not appear as sweetness in the mouth; a similar experience can happen with an Alsace gewurztraminer, when the rose petals, Turkish Delight, or lychees on the nose cannot be tasted, more's the pity. Indeed, these experiences demonstrate why anyone drinking wine should sniff before sipping: the pleasure is doubled. In short, winespeak can take you only so far: after that it is up to you—unless, of course, you always follow your guru, no matter where he leads.

Must you have a guru?

IN THE WORLD of wine, both amateur and professional, there is probably no stronger source of conflict than the rating and ranking of wines. Professional reputations are involved, as are the livelihoods of producers, brokers and wine merchants in various parts of the world. There are a variety of systems, some of which claim an objectivity and precision that supporters of other systems deride as impossible. There is certainly a split between the United States and Europe, which is exacerbated by the scorn occasionally poured on each side by the other. The poor consumer, who is looking for guidance, is left confused.

Undoubtedly the most influential wine taster in the world is Robert Parker, whose *The Wine Advocate* has a readership of thousands. His driving motive was indeed to help the poor consumer to find out more about a wine than could be gleaned from reading the label. His approach is to buy his own bottles or to taste from the barrels, sniff, sip, slosh it around his mouth, and quickly reach his verdict. His method is preeminently by snap-shot, and while he often returns and retastes a wine a year or two later, it is usually too late for any change in his opin-ion to have much effect on the market. His tasting abilities are almost universally acknowledged to be phenomenal, but the perception is that he homes in on certain types of wine: heavily extracted, alcoholic, less acidic, and with "gobs of fruit"—what one female somme-lier has referred to as "penis wines." He is accused of having driven many wine producers to skew their winemaking methods in order to create so-called Parker wines, wines that he is likely to rate highly and which as a result will be swept up by eager customers.

Parker's scoring system—used by American schools and colleges—is based on a maximum of 100 points. However, the scoring effectively begins at 50: as one fellow taster said, a wine gets 50 points "just for showing up." Thereafter:

> **50–64:** *to be avoided*
> **65–74:** *average*
> **75–79:** *above average*
> **80–89:** *very good*
> **90–95:** *outstanding*
> **96–100:** *extraordinary*

Parker has always insisted that customers should look at his tasting notes, not merely at the numbers, but the extent to which most of them do so is questionable. The thing is, for Americans, these numbers trigger off deeply held memories: at school, 90–100 was an A to A+, 80–89 a B, 70–79 a C, 60–69 a D, and then you fell off the cliff and your parents either yelled at you or, worse, looked deeply disappointed. In short, many Americans respond to the simplicity and familiarity and, convinced by

Parker's rock-hard certainty that he is accurate, place their wine bets on his choices. Presumably they also follow him because they like the wines he praises.

In Britain, the situation is very different. Granted that British universities also give marks out of 100, nevertheless, receiving anything higher than an 85 is rare in any discipline that requires continuous prose, as opposed to mathematics or languages. Therefore, the idea of a 100-point "perfect" wine seems risible. British critics have traditionally depended on descriptions of wines rather than on numbers, and the quality of the prose of a number of them is part of the pleasure of reading about the wines. Nevertheless, each has his or her system. Hugh Johnson, editor of the eponymous *Pocket Wine Book*, assesses producers or areas rather than individual wines:

> *—Plain, everyday quality
> **—Above average
> ***—Well-known, highly reputed
> ****—Grand, prestigious, expensive

Tongue in cheek, he also offers the following somewhat idiosyncratic system to his readers:

> ONE SNIFF: *the minimum score; emphatically no thanks*
> ONE SIP: *one step up*
> TWO SIPS: *faint interest (or disbelief)*
> A HALF GLASS: *slight hesitation*
> ONE GLASS: *tolerance, even general approval*
> TWO GLASSES: *means you quite like it (or there is nothing else to drink)*
> THREE GLASSES: *you find it more than acceptable*
> FOUR GLASSES: *it tickles your fancy*
> ONE BOTTLE: *means satisfaction*

A SECOND BOTTLE: *is the real thumbs-up*
A FULL DOZEN: *means you are not going to miss out on this one*

The logical top score in the Johnson system is the whole vine-yard.

The ratings given by wine magazines can also be influential, and they, too, have their own systems. The scores from the American magazine *Wine Spectator* are frequently cited on slips under bottles in wine shops. It, too, uses the 100-point system, which Parker's influence has established as the normal American way of rating wines. The British magazine *Decanter* has a hybrid system, using both stars and, latterly, a 20-point system, thereby providing an indication for some and certitude for others. It is certainly easier to remember stars than decimals:

*/ 10.5–12.49—*Poor*
**/12.5–14.49—*Fair*
***/14.5–16.49—*Recommended*
****/16.5–18.49—*Highly recommended*
*****/18.5–20—*Outstanding*

What is probably the most intelligently nuanced system, however, is that provided by the international magazine *The World of Fine Wine*, which also uses a 20-point scale:

0–7: *Disagreeable or faulty wine*
7.5–10: *Sound but dull or boring wine of no character or appeal*
10.5–12: *Enjoyable, simple and straightforward wine*
12.5–14: *Good wine, but with no outstanding features*
14.5–16.5: *Very good wine, with some outstanding features*
17–18.5: *Outstanding wine of great beauty and articulacy*
19–20: *A great wine, of spellbinding beauty and resonance, leaving the drinker with a sense of wonder*

It should be pointed out that the Parker effect is limited to a narrow range of wines, primarily those of Bordeaux and the Rhône, although a number of the wines of Burgundy, the assessment of which Parker now largely leaves to others, have also benefited. But most other areas look in vain for much attention, with, of course, the overwhelmingly important exception of California, where the Parker effect has been at least as striking as for Bordeaux.

But what Parker ascertained very early on, and what other critics have had to adopt to a greater or lesser extent, is the requirement for some precision in rating and ranking wines. It does not much matter if you believe that wines change and evolve, that wines vary from bottle to bottle, that judgment is just that, a human judgment, not an edict from heaven: customers look for help and firm guidance, and critics and writers feel that they must give it to them. It is all very well to say that you must taste the wine yourself and make your own judgment, but for many wine drinkers, who have not had the advantage of tasting thousands of wines, going into a shop and facing row upon row of bottles can be daunting.

To answer the question, then: most wine drinkers feel at least the occasional need for some guidance from a person whose taste they trust. The more experienced will have built up their own sense of what they like and which wines they prefer to drink, but they might still hope to have their preferences confirmed. The point is, there are a number of systems and gurus out there, and you can choose the one whose choices tend to point you toward wines you enjoy. Those who collect rather than drink will always find a Parker indispensable: not only will he say what wines are the best and should be bought, but the power of his scores ensures that there will be stimulating competition to get those wines. He provides a level playing field for that particular game, which the rest of us can watch while marveling at human nature.

They drank *how much* at a sitting?

IN HIS WONDERFUL book on eighteenth-century London, *City of Laughter*, the historian Vic Gatrell quotes La Rochefoucauld's experiences of the Duke of Grafton's hospitality at Euston Hall in London. "The drinking is sometimes quite alarming," the French aphorist wrote:

> The bottles go continually round the table, and the master of the house makes sure that no one misses a turn . . . the conversation could hardly be freer; everyone gives his political opinions with the same ease as his opinions on personal matters. Sometimes the conversation becomes equally free on indecent matters, for one is allowed to speak of everything . . . I have heard things said here in good company that would be the worst breach of decent manners in France.

He goes on to quote another Frenchman, Faujas de Saint-Fond, who is shocked by the inevitable chamber pot, used "with so little ceremony that the person who has occasion to use it does not even interrupt his talk during the operation."

We may be shocked, too, but we can hardly be surprised when we realize that a man might drink three bottles of wine at dinner and think nothing of it. Pitt the Younger—described bawdily as "stiff to everybody but a lady"—would drink a bottle of port at home before going into the House of Commons, then share a couple more with his friend Dundas afterward. The Duke of York drank so much that "six bottles of claret after dinner scarcely made a perceptible change in his countenance." Byron, Gatrell tells us, would drink from six in the evening until five the next morning, and on it went.

How things have changed. Scarcely a day passes, it seems, without the modern citizen being scolded and admonished and warned about the evils of drink. It would not seem so bad if there were any reason or consistency to it, but one moment doctors tell us that any wine at all will surely do for us, the next that a glass, or two units (did anyone ever say to another, "Do you fancy popping out for a few units?" we wonder), or whatever is the currently fashionable amount will protect us from heart disease. Actually, no, it won't. No—as you were. It will. But only if it's red. Nope, sorry, doesn't matter if it's red or not, it'll kill you . . .

It would seem even more patronizing had the cat not been let out of the bag that the U.K. government's "recommended weekly unit consumption" was imaginary. By "imaginary" we mean that it had been made up. There was no scientific basis for it at all. They had plucked the figures from thin air.

Recently we were told that it was the unemployed and undereducated who were most at risk from alcohol. Even more recently, we were told, no, it was the middle classes who were *really* at risk. Most recently of all (at the time of writing; who knows what will happen hereafter), the Royal College of Physicians claimed that pubs are "pushing customers towards unsafe levels of drinking" by selling wine in big glasses, and an MP who is of course not being opportunist to increase his profile (which is why we are not going to name him) demanded a new law to make them stop it and sell us little glasses instead.

We have only two comments to make. Well, actually, we have *three* comments to make, but we will only be allowed to make two of them. The first is that the people who roam around inner cities at night, roaring, vomiting, and fighting, are not usually those who have been drinking a rather nice pinot noir in whatever size of glass. And the second is that someone who cannot tell whether they are holding a big glass of wine or a little glass of wine should not really be allowed to hold any glass at all, and certainly not one with wine in.

We live in stern and pursed-lipped times. The reign of Dionysos, god of wine, of fertility, of ecstasies and collective joy, is quite o'erthrown. In his place stands political Apollo: virtuous, controlled, ordered, and orderly. Perhaps we should all get together over a bottle or two and see if we can't find a middle way . . .

What is a connoisseur?

THE QUESTION IS perfectly answered in the definition, and example, given by Ambrose Bierce in *The Devil's Dictionary*, and nothing else needs to be said:

> CONNOISSEUR, n. A specialist who knows everything about something and nothing about anything else.
>
> An old wine-bibber having been smashed in a railway collision, some wine was poured on his lips to revive him. "Pauillac, 1873," he murmured, and died.

BIBLIOGRAPHY

"Food scientist finds line separating fruit and vegetable wine from 'plonk.'" *Cornell Chronicle*, September 3, 1998, http://www.news.cornell.edu/chronicle/98/9.3.98/fruit-veg_wine.html (accessed April 14, 2008)

"The truth about impotence." *Nova Magazine*, http://www.pbs.org/wgbh/nova/impotence/questions/transcript.html (accessed April 10, 2008)

Allen, H. Warner. *A History of Wine: Great Vintage Wines from the Homeric Age to the Present Day* (Faber and Faber, 1961)

Bierce, Ambrose. *The Devil's Dictionary* (Bloomsbury, 2003)

Bird, David. *Understanding Wine Technology* (2nd ed.) (DBQA Publications, 2005)

Brewer, David J. "An Independent Judiciary as the Salvation of the Nation." *Proceedings of the New York State Bar Association*, 37, 37–47 (1893)

Broadbent, Michael. *Vintage Wines* (Little, Brown, 2002)

Brook, Stephen. *The Wines of Germany* (Mitchell Beazley, 2003)

Burk, Kathleen. Accumulated knowledge

Burr, Chandler. *The Emperor of Scent: A Story of Perfume, Obsession and the Last Mystery of the Senses* (Heinemann, 2003)

Clark, Alan. *Diaries* (Weidenfeld & Nicolson, 1993)

Clarke, Oz. *Pocket Wine Book* (Pavilion Books, annual)

David, Elizabeth. *French Provincial Cooking* (Penguin, 1970)

———. *An Omelette and a Glass of Wine* (Penguin, 1986)

Davidson, James. *Courtesans and Fishcakes: The Consuming Passions of Classical Athens* (HarperCollins, 1997)

Emsley, John. *The Elements of Murder: A History of Poison* (Oxford University Press, 2005)

European Council Regulation (EC) No 1493/1999 of 17 May 1999 on the Common regulation of the market in wine

Faith, Nicholas. *The Winemasters of Bordeaux: The Inside Story of the World's Greatest Wines* (Prion, 1999)

Fermor, Patrick Leigh. *Between the Woods and the Water* (Penguin, 1988)

———. *A Time of Gifts: On Foot to Constantinople—From the Hook of Holland to the Middle Danube* (Penguin, 1979)

Flower, Raymond. *The Palace: A Profile of St. Moritz* (Debrett, 1982)

———. *Chianti: The Land, the People and the Wine* (revised ed.) (Christopher Helm, 1988)

Gatrell, Vic. *City of Laughter: Sex and Satire in Eighteenth-Century London* (Atlantic, 2007)

Goode, Jamie. "Beauty and the Beast—Premature Oxidation." *The World of Fine Wine*, 14, 88–92 (2006)

———. *Wine Science* (Octopus Publishing, 2005)

Gryn, Jo. "Decanting: Is it Useful?" *The World of Fine Wine*, 19, 86–89 (2008)

Harding, Graham. *A Wine Miscellany* (Michael O'Mara Books, 2005)

Harris, Robert. *Pompeii* (Hutchinson, 2003)

Healy, Maurice. *Stay Me With Flagons: A Book About Wine and Other Things* (Michael Joseph, 1949)

Homer. *The Iliad*, trans. Andrew Lang et al. (London, 1883)

Jakob, Friedrich. *Die grosse Orgel der Basilika zu Weingarten* (Männedorf, 1986)

Jewess, Michael, unpublished research on temperature reequilibration of wine in domestic environments (2008)

Johnson, Hugh. *Pocket Wine Book* (Mitchell Beazley, annual)

———. *Story of Wine* (Mitchell Beazley, 1989)

———. *Wine: A Life Uncorked* (Weidenfeld & Nicolson, 2005)

Kalev-Zylinska, Maggie L., and Matthew J. During. "Paradoxical Facilitatory Effect of Low-Dose Alcohol Consumption on Memory Mediated by NMDA Receptors." *The Journal of Neuroscience*, September 26, 2007, 27(39):10456–10467

Kay, Billy, and Cailean Maclean. *Knee Deep in Claret: A Celebration of Wine and Scotland* (Mainstream, 1983)

Kirkup, James. "Low-alcohol wine to help cut drinking." *Daily Telegraph* (London), March 25, 2008

Kline, Morris. *Mathematical Thought from Ancient to Modern Times*, Vol. 1 (Oxford University Press, 1972)

Lynd, Robert. *Dr. Johnson & Company* (Penguin, 1946)

McCoy, Elin. *The Emperor of Wine: The Rise of Robert M. Parker, Jr. and the Reign of American Taste* (HarperCollins, 2005)

McGovern, Patrick E. *Ancient Wine: The Search for the Origins of Viticulture* (Princeton University Press, 2003)

Mayr, Johannes. *Joseph Gabler, Orgelmacher* (Biberach, 2000)

Mayson, Richard. *Port and the Douro* (Faber and Faber, 1999)

Merck Manual of Geriatrics. http://www.merck.com/mkgr/mmg/sec14/ch115/ch115b.jsp (accessed April 10, 2008)

Plato. *The Symposium*, trans. Walter Hamilton (Penguin, 1951)

Pliny. *Natural History*, trans. H. Rackham, Books 12-16 (Harvard University Press, 1968)

Pliny the Younger. *Complete Letters*, trans. P. G. Walsh (Oxford University Press, 2006)

Porter, Roy, and G. S. Rousseau. *Gout: The Patrician Malady* (Yale University Press, 2000)

Robinson, Jancis. *The Oxford Companion to Wine* (3rd ed.) (Oxford University Press, 2006)

———. *Vines, Grapes and Wines* (Mitchell Beazley, 1992)

Roxanne's Wine Cellar. http://scorpius.spaceports.com/~goodwine (accessed April 14, 2008)

Simon, André L. *The History of the Wine Trade in England*, Vol. 2 (Holland Press, 1964)

Skelton, Stephen. *The Wines of Britain and Ireland* (Faber and Faber, 2001)

Spargo, John Webster. "Clarence in the Malmsey-Butt." *Modern Language Notes*, 51(3), 166–73 (1936)

Sun, Lau Chi. "Ancient Chinese Wine Poetry." *The World of Fine Wine*, 10, 62–65 (2006)

Süskind, Patrick. *Perfume: The Story of a Murderer* (Penguin, 2006)

Symonds, John Addington. *Wine, Women and Song* (Chatto & Windus, 1884)

Waller, John. *The Discovery of the Germ* (Icon Books, 2002)

Weinreib, Tzvi Hersh. "It is not a mitzvah to get drunk on Purim." The Orthodox Union, March 15, 2005. http://www.ou.org/oupr/2005/purimoped65.htm (accessed April 12, 2008)

Younger, William. *Gods, Men, and Wine* (Michael Joseph, 1966)

INDEX

NOTE ON THE INDEX: We have followed the Master of Wine style in which grape *varietals* are capitalized but the *generic wines* are not. Hence Chardonnay (the grape) but chardonnay (the wine). Individual wines, generic or otherwise, are indexed under "wines." Where appropriate, the "Château" designation has been removed. So, not "Château Mouton-Rothschild" but just "Mouton-Rothschild."